BEWARE OF BEAUTIFUL DAYS

PREQUEL TO THE JACK CURTIS MYSTERIES

TRISHA HUGHES

PREVIOUSLY BY THE AUTHOR

Autobiography

Daughters of Nazareth

Historical Fiction

Book 1

Vikings to Virgin – *The Story of England's Monarchs from The Vikings to The Virgin Queen*

Book 2

Virgin to Victoria – *The Story of England's Monarchs from The Virgin Queen to Queen Victoria*

Book 3

Victoria to Vikings - *The Circle of Blood*

The Story of England's Monarchs from Queen Victoria to The Vikings

The Tartan Kings - *A Powerful & Rich Story of Scotland*

Crime/Mystery

Dragonfly

Chameleon

Scorpion

Copyright

The characters and events in this book are fictitious.
Any similarity to real persons, living or dead, is coincidental and not intended by the author.
All rights reserved. No part of this publication may be reproduced, distributed or transmitted in any form or by any means without the prior written permission of the author.

Copyright © 2024 Trisha Hughes

The right of Trisha Hughes to be identified as the author of this work has been asserted by her in accordance with
The Copyright, Designs and Patents Act 1988

CONTACT THE AUTHOR

Contact the author at
trisha.hughes.books@gmail.com
For updates and discounts on new releases,
join Trisha Hughes mailing list at
https://www.trishahughesauthor.com/contact

1

If I had one wish, it would be the ability to catch a glimpse of the future and what lies ahead. We might see things that make no sense whatsoever and some, I suppose, would scare the hell out of us. If we knew what was coming, we could avoid certain choices and mistakes and select a different fork in the road that would change our future. If we only knew, we could exercise discretion and restructure our fate. But we're shielded from the knowledge of these dangers ahead and this means, you could say, we're protected from future horrors. At some point in our lives, we all want to go back in time for some reason or other. It has to do with the illusion of control that we all want to use against helplessness in a world that we can't really control. But I guess there are no guarantees in life and rubbish gets thrown at all of us at some time in their lives. How we deal with that rubbish is who we are.

Hindsight is a wonderful thing. When I look back now on that Monday I ask myself *'What if I hadn't gone to work that day.' 'What if I'd had one more week off like my doctor had told me to do?'* If I'd only done one of those two things, I wouldn't have been sitting in my car watching the medical crew cut the body down after he'd tried to hang himself in a deserted lane off Marine Parade. Mixed in with the smell of sea salt and seaweed, the wind carried the smell of McMeals, exhaust fumes, alcohol, coconut oil and excrement.

You didn't have to be a genius to know that the guy had been drinking heavily and had changed his mind about ending his life at the last minute. Most of his fingernails were broken and bloodied from clawing at the rope around his neck and the toes on one foot were broken from kicking at the wall. But by then it had been too late. At the end, he'd shown such a desperate will to live, that it made me wonder what had preceded the suicide act. Where was the determination to live as he put the cord around his neck?

I'm not one those people who believes in fate or karma but the strange thing is, before heading off to work that morning, I'd had an unsettling feeling in the pit of my stomach, an uneasiness, but I put it down to my first day back at work after a long break. It was, after all, 1st January. Any cop will tell you that New Year's Day has always been a big day for depression and suicides. While most people view New Year's Day with a sense of hope for a better year than the last one, there were those who see it as a good day on which to die. There'd be no happy-ever-afters for this guy.

I glanced down at my watch and made a note of the time in my notebook for when I wrote up my report later on at the station. It was right on 12 o'clock and if I was lucky, my day was halfway through. In just four hours, I'd been called to a botched armed hold-up at a convenience store and two suicides. I put the notebook back in my jacket lying on the passenger seat of my car and looked back up through my windscreen just as the body was being loaded onto a stretcher and wheeled unceremoniously into the coroner's van that was crammed into the quiet lane behind the blue crime scene tape stretched across the street. Behind the tape stood reporters, shuffling their feet and standing at the ready with microphones trying to catch my attention, eagerness written all over their faces. From where I stood, I could see a female reporter had snared a local woman and was asking her questions with concern written all over on her face. TV gold.

"You don't expect anything bad to happen here. Not here." The quivering words drifted over to me as the reporter arranged her features into a perfect blend of sympathy and shock for the camera. Those drama lessons at school hadn't been wasted after all.

She flicked her blonde hair back from her shoulders and waited for the woman to stop blowing her nose before continuing.

The heat was already brutal and as I watched, one hand shielding the sun against my eyes, I could feel wet patches under my arms and an itch in my crotch. Body odour wafted up from my armpits, fighting against the cloying scent of my aftershave. By lunchtime in this weather, the hospitals would be full of people suffering from heatstroke, sunburn and God knows how many victims of testosterone-induced fights exacerbated by the heat.

Thankfully at that point in my morbid thoughts, my mobile rang, turning my thoughts away from the scene before me. I looked at the number and smiled a little.

"Welcome back, Jack," the female voice sing-songed on the other end of the line.

The voice was Sam Neil's or rather, Detective Samantha Neil. It was clear and teasing, and in my mind, I saw the lop-sided smile, the chocolate-brown eyes and the little lines that crinkled at the corners of her eyes.

I hadn't been at work for six weeks due to a bullet to the mid-section. My doctor assured me I'd made a full recovery, but to be honest, it had frightened me to think I'd come *this* close to death although I feel compelled to state that, unlike most reports about the moment of death, my life did not pass before my eyes in a flash. There was no bright light at the end of a dark tunnel, no warm fuzzy feeling that heralded my approach to the other side. What I *did* hear was a little voice in my head saying in an outraged tone, *'You've got to be kidding me! This is it?'* Where were my dearly departed relatives and friends who were supposed to welcome me over to the other side? And where were the angels? All I saw was the waves crashing over the sand and a few scraggly seagulls flying overhead.

Because of the forced leave, I'd been feeling restless and bored listening to the day-to-day routine of my neighbours. I hadn't had a break from work in five years and I was like a reformed drunk whose hand reaches for the bottle looking for a fix that isn't there anymore. For almost thirteen years, I have been a part of an organisation that promotes isolation from the outside world and all of a sudden, I'd been temporarily *in* that 'outside' world with no idea how to act because I really wasn't part of *their* club.

So here I was, glad to be back at work two weeks earlier than the doctors had recommended, giving someone the opportunity for some unexpected time off. As for me, I couldn't put up with the boredom at home another day.

"You finished out there yet?" she chirped.

That's the only way to describe Sam's voice. Chirpy. She was dark-haired with a little Irish perhaps in the background somewhere and she was chirpy. But this Sam Neil did not look like the Sam Neil from Hollywood. This one stood at 5 feet 4 inches tall and although she clearly preferred wearing lightweight skirt suits, she couldn't hide the gentle curves that were plainly obvious beneath the fabric. Apart from being nice on the eye, the best thing you can hope for is a partner like Sam Neil. I'd missed her for the past six weeks.

"Almost," I replied as I watched the coroner's blue van pull away into traffic. "The 'tag 'em and bag 'em' team are just leaving." I watched the coroner's blue van in silence as it pulled away into traffic before saying, "Please don't tell me you've got something else for me."

"Sorry, Jack. I thought I'd call you rather than put it out over the radio. All we need today is the media to pick this one up."

"How come you were rostered for today?' I asked. "Did you piss off someone or are you just having a fight with your husband?"

As soon as I uttered the words, I wished I could take them back. The rumour at the station was that she and her husband were having marital problems. Like most cops, there was a fine balance between work and home life and if we were all honest about it, we'd admit that work took precedence every time. Ask my ex-wife.

Instead of a mild reproof, she said, "Jack. Could I let you come back to work on your first day without being here to welcome you?"

Her voice sounded teasing and with a certain degree of relief, I mumbled, "Yeah, well, where are all the dancing girls then?"

"It's a public holiday, Jack. You'll have to make do with me".

I was already regretting I'd ignored the doctor's advice to stay at home. "Just tell me it's not another suicide," I complained. "I've had my fair share today."

"Nope. Not a suicide. Someone on the road to Tamborine Mountain was out walking his dog and called in to say it had come running back with a bone in its mouth. He says it's human and it's an arm bone."

I almost groaned. You get these calls from time to time and they're always hysteria based. Usually there's a simple explanation and most times, the bones turn out to be animal bones. But these days, people watch CSI and overnight everyone's an expert.

As if she'd been reading my mind, she said, "I know what you're thinking, Jack. Not another bone run. But this is different. The guy with the dog? He's a doctor. And he says he's absolutely positive it's a humerus and it's from a child. He says...hang on...' I heard paper rustling over the earpiece as Sam began reading from her notes. "Here we are. In his statement, he says the bone's got a visible fracture just above the elbow. The... ummm...medial epicondyle."

I felt a trickle of electric current run down the back of my neck. One day back and I was straight into a case with no time to catch my breath. I knew I wasn't going to be at my best after six weeks of drinking beer and lazing in a recliner on my veranda, but it was good to feel the old familiar rush nonetheless.

"I'm reading from my notes here, Jack, so I'm not sure if that's the right pronunciation. But the doctor says it definitely from a child. I've got the address here."

"Hang on. Let me get something to write it down."

I did a balancing act with my mobile phone, holding it in the crook of my neck between my ear and my shoulder as I opened the notebook. "By the way," I said as I leant on the roof of my car, "you were right to keep it off the air, Sam. The last thing we need is reporters wandering all over the crime scene before we even get there."

A hot breeze picked up down the alley, blowing the pages of the notepad, but I managed to place my elbow on the pad while still holding the phone in place. "Okay, go ahead. Where do you want me to go?"

She gave me a Mount Tamborine address and finished up by saying she'd meet me there with a team.

I ended the call and glanced over to the entrance of the lane where the body had been found. My bet was we wouldn't find any next of kin and he would be treated the same way in death as he had been treated in life. Left alone and forgotten.

I stood for a second longer, looking around and listening to the silence before getting in my car. It looked depressing and abandoned. Just the promise of another scorcher in Paradise. I indicated and pulled away from the curb, heading towards Mount Tamborine.

What I didn't know was that within one week, my life and my world would spiral out of control and change irrevocably forever.

2

Beware of beautiful days. Bad things seem to happen on beautiful days. The two suicides had been my signposts but I'd ignored the warnings, focusing instead on the chance of investigating a possible murder. I thought the suicides were as bad as the day was going to get but as it turned out, I was very wrong. I had no warning, not one single moment, of what was about to occur. That's the way big things happen in your life.

Crime has always existed throughout history and it knows no boundaries. It exists in all cultures, committed by all races and in all time periods. But it was hard to believe it that morning as I breathed in the salty tang of the ocean after winding down my car window to let in the breathtaking morning sun. The sky over Surfers Paradise was a deep, sharp blue, washed clean of dirt and chemical elements after last night's thunderstorm and it was as pure as I've ever seen it.

I remember the day was one of those exceptionally beautiful summer days that nearly stops your heart. It was still one month away from what was officially autumn and I was looking forward to waking with the sun's gentle warmth on my face instead of scorching heat Surfers Paradise was suffering through. If you've never visited Queensland in the summertime, more precisely the Gold Coast, you can only imagine what the heat is like at this time of year. Despite that, when Nature throws in a sea breeze, it's no wonder the world believes we live in Paradise.

At times on the Gold Coast, it's easy to believe that you're living on a movie set. It looks real but somehow you can't quite believe that so much beauty exists in one place. 80 kms to the north lay Queensland's capital Brisbane and to the west in the distance, hazy hills gradually transformed into a tableland called Tamborine Mountain. Further on, they became the proper mountain range of the Great Dividing Range separating us from the farming and grazing area of the Darling Downs.

What never ceases to amaze me is that whether it's winter or summer, you can always expect magnificent blue skies and the endless starry nights. Then, without forewarning, the heavens seem to have a fit, exploding with thunder and lightening and washing away the smoke from the bush fires, leaving behind crystal blue skies the colour of topaz. That's the way it is in this city. Heat then rain. Rain then heat again.

If you can get past the humidity, you'll find Surfers is a beautiful place. Sometimes, the humidity is so high; the moist air makes you feel like you're breathing water. That's when people head down to the beach. On any public holiday or weekend in summer, there are lines of traffic headed for the coast on the M1 from Brisbane. They get here to the Gold Coast very slowly and return at a quarter of the pace. Some people head off to public swimming pools, which in my opinion, are about one-half chlorine and the other half screaming kids, while others dress in faded boardshorts and t-shirts and stand shoulder to shoulder in air-conditioned pubs and drink the day away. Then you get the melanoma candidates who strip off and soak up the nuclear heat on the beach as they slowly roast themselves to a turn. What amazes me is that for as far as the eye can see, there never seems to be any orange-peel bums squeezed into their miniscule bikinis. There might not be much good in this world but show me anyone who has a bad thing to say about bikinis and I'll show you a lunatic.

That Monday, traffic was light but I still caught every red light possible. The asphalt glittered in the sun and it felt hot enough to fry an egg on the bitumen. The sky was a deep, sharp blue, washed clean of dirt and chemical elements that sometimes colours the skies after a storm. The air smelt of the sea as white seagulls circled overhead eyeing the McDonald's and Kentucky Fried parking lots for leftovers. Shirtless young men and girls with ponytails walked along the sidewalks overlooking the dazzling ocean while shopkeepers set up stands outside their shops ready for the tourists in the late afternoon. Palm trees swayed and the nutty smell of coconut oil wafted in the gentle breeze. Everyone was smiling as the sun glistened off the ocean like it was jam-packed with diamonds. At this time of morning, people selling dope weren't noticeable, but maybe I wasn't looking closely enough.

You see, it was a beautiful day.

I dropped into a McDonald's drive-through and bought a large fries and a coke to have on the way, knowing this was going to be all I'd have time for. As I sat in the traffic lights staring at the ocean and eating the fries, cars, trucks and buses stretched ahead as far as I could see, moving forward slowly when the traffic lights changed, then coming to a halt again while more traffic flowed across the intersection. A shadow flitted across my windscreen and I heard the rhythmic 'whup-whup-whup' of the rotor blades from a helicopter as it sped across the sky on its way to Seaworld on the Spit. Close to Seaworld, I knew people would be having their first glass of wine with lunch at The Marina Mirage or the Versace resort. As I tapped my fingers on the steering wheel in time to the music coming from my speakers, it was easy to believe in magic. As Surfers Paradise bustled around me, I was secure in my ignorance of the terrible things to come.

With the windows opened, the effect was like sitting in a fan-forced oven and I could feel sweat trickling down my back leaving an itching trail in its wake. I wound the window back up and switched the air-conditioning on and settled in for the half-hour drive up the winding road to Tamborine Mountain.

****

The drive started off pleasantly enough but ended up steep as I threaded my way around the mountain and through the bushland towards the rainforest at the top. I kept my speedometer on a steady 40 kms an hour around the curves and took in the scenery.

If you've read the brochures of Tamborine Mountain, you'll know that it's the showcase of the Gold Coast and *oozes* charm. It's situated 70 kms south of Brisbane and 25 kms inland from Surfers Paradise. It's flat-topped and rises 580 metres above the surrounding countryside and is the home for about 6,000 residents who share it with tourists visiting the wineries, breweries, B & B's, bush walks and markets, both craft and produce.

All seemed pretty quiet but to me the air buzzed with a nervousness it gets when the wind begins to blow, dry as a bone, cooking the hillsides into kindling that can snap into flames hot enough to melt a car chassis. The air smelt of smoke and a column of smoke rose off towards a distant ridge line where the Gold Coast City Council were conducting 'controlled burning' to halt the devastation that happens around this time every year. When it does happen, it's big news. Despite the flames and the heat, news choppers dive close enough to ignite because next to terrorist activity and whatever Nicole Kidman was currently doing, fires are our largest spectator sport.

Unlike the open grasslands, the Tamborine Valley looked lush and green. The low foliage glowed a deep, luscious green while thick coarse vines wound themselves around trees in their attempt to reach the sun. Despite my windows being wound up, the sweet, cloying odour of eucalyptus along with a musky animal smell drifted in.

I'm not a nature lover myself but driving through the dappled light filtering through the trees and listening to the cacophony of birds, I have to tell you, I was pretty impressed.

The road continued over an old wooden bridge crossing a stream before my GPS directions told me to take a dead-end tributary off the main road into a heavily wooded area. I sighed audibly knowing that searching for bones in this area would only end up becoming a nightmare.

Real estate material refers to this area as a *'sparkling jewel in a parklike setting'* and the views are always described as *'breathtaking'*, *'stunning'*, or *'spectacular'*. Words like *'serenity'* and *'tranquillity'* abound. Every noun has an adjective attached to give it the proper tone and substance. The *'lush, well-manicured'* lots are large and the *'elegant, spacious'* homes are set well away from the roads and *'dotted'* with palms amid tropical gardens. Lots of *'dotteds'* and *'amids'*.

I pulled to a stop beside a patrol car and noticed a blue Subaru parked outside the address Sam had given me. I checked my watch before writing the time down on my duty sheet, noting it was 1.35 pm. At this time of year, I had about 4½ hours of good sunlight left.

An 8-foot-high stone wall, overgrown with trailing ivy, separated the house from the road. It followed the street uphill before disappearing over the rise. Eucalyptus trees and melaleucas, gnarled, grey and well-established, lined the wall both inside and outside the wall, which probably meant they were here before I was born. Through the gate, the path disappeared around a bend.

I eased myself out of my car, groaning as I unfolded my body and protecting my healing wound while taking in the surrounding area. From where I was standing, I couldn't see the house. I couldn't see *anything* because the trees were so thick, making everything look gloomy. Here I was, in the middle of a hot summer's day at 1.30 in the afternoon, and it was so dark and quiet, it felt ominous. It made me feel like I was a kid sneaking out to do something bad and not wanting anyone to hear or see me. This place did that to you. It was so quiet the ticking of the car's cooling engine sounded like finger snaps and I made a mental note to carry a crucifix and a sharpened wooden stake the next time I had to come here.

My usual routine is to stand for a few moments and let the surroundings speak to me. A friend of mine once said that you can tell how a person is on the inside by noticing what they create around them on the outside. Having said that, it doesn't always work. For example, only a couple of years ago, I was called to a crime scene where an old guy had been murdered. His rented room reeked of dirty clothes and decaying food. If I hadn't known why they'd locked up Barry Nesbitt three years ago and only just released him, I'd have said, 'Poor bugger, and only out of gaol.' That is until I looked under the bed and saw the shoe box full of photos of pre-pubescent kids and the Kmart catalogue with its photographs of children in their pyjamas and underwear that I knew he wasn't looking at for fashion tips for his kids.

I sighed and stretched my back trying to ease the uncomfortable feeling in my stomach that still came when I sat too long in one spot. For all my griping, keeping active was by far a better option than a lot of desk work because I knew the pain would only get worse if I sat still for too long.

The clear sky was streaked with wispy strips of residual smoke but otherwise it was like a sheet of stainless steel spray-painted blue and I blinked against the brassy sun in my eyes. If I didn't make a move soon I'd be a puddle. As I blinked, Sam stepped out of the Subaru and walked around it towards me in four-inch heels. As she swayed towards me, I couldn't help but admire her balance in them. Her soft eyes regarded me quietly. As a greeting, she grunted.

I raised an eyebrow at her as I wiped a trickle of sweat off the end of my nose.

"Is that the best you can do after six weeks?" I asked in mock reproof. "A grunt? Did Scully grunt at Mulder? Did Lois Lane grunt at Superman?"

She smiled her lopsided smile at me as she looked me up and down.

"Did you pay money for that tie?"

"And a good afternoon to you too, Sam. Do you want this knife back or should I just keep it here in my heart?" I said as I shook my head forlornly.

She smiled wider. "Come on, old man, follow me."

As she began walking towards the house, gravel crunching under her feet, I fell into step beside her.

"Can you believe this day? My first day back on the job. Wouldn't you think they'd let me snooze in the squad room for a few days and let me ease back slowly?"

She kept walking but said nothing.

I glanced at her reprovingly. "A little sensitivity and compassion wouldn't go astray right now, you know."

She turned and smiled widely at me. "Oh Jack. Are you feeling a little unloved today?"

"Just being my charming self."

The front door opened up to the back of the house, running into a room where a uniformed policeman stood with his arms crossed over his chest. Sitting at a cluttered desk was a middle-aged man with wavy brown hair parted in the middle that was touching his shoulders. His chinos had seen better days and the worn t-shirt told me he was probably on welfare. I couldn't see his shoes but I was betting he wasn't wearing any. I was beginning to wonder if I needed to send some beat cops out to scrounge around for traces of marijuana. Lying beside him on the floor was a large yellow dog of indiscriminate breeds.

The man looked up at me with sharp blue eyes and instantly stood up.

He was over six foot tall and could not be called a soft man but at the same time there was no muscle or definition of his body.

I held out my hand and said, "Good afternoon. I'm Sergeant Curtis, sir."

He shook my hand and said, "Doctor Philipe Germain."

His French accent was thick and smooth, the sort that sends members of the female gender into a swoon. Without any such help, I have to depend on my rugged good looks and charming personality to win women over. Which is probably why I live alone with a cat.

The man glanced up at me with sharp eyes the colour of the sky on a soft winter's morning, and instantly stood up.

He was over six feet and could not be called a soft man but at the same time there was no muscle or definition of his body.

"Nice to meet you," I muttered.

He nodded back and I swear I saw the hint of a smile.

"This is it?" I asked looking down at what was a weathered bone that had the look of a piece of driftwood resting on a tea towel on the desk.

"That is your bone, Sergeant. Yes. As you can see...." he reached over to a book by his elbow and opened it to a previously marked spot, "this bone is definitely a humerus from a small child."

The page showed an illustrated picture of a bone, anterior and posterior views, and a sketch of a skeleton with the humerus bones of both arms was highlighted with an orange marker.

He gently lifted the bone and held it against the book's illustration and went through a point-by-point comparison.

He raised his eyes to mine. "It is all there. I have been telling your partner here," he glanced over towards Sam, "I know my bones without having to look them up in a book but it is good for you to have a reference. No?"

I nodded slowly. "Do you have a clinic here, Doctor?"

He straightened his back slightly. "No, but that does not mean that I don't recognise a human bone when I......"

I tried to smile and held up a hand to placate him. "I didn't mean to question you, doctor. I believe you. If you say it's a humerus, then it's a humerus. I'm just trying to get a picture here of everything."

He gently placed the bone back on the tea towel silently.

"What's your dog's name?" I asked.

"Caesar," he said, bending down and ruffling the dog's head.

Caesar was a mess of a dog, a concoction slapped together by a blind Frankenstein complete with a shaggy coat, a whip of a tail and dripping drool. If the Raman Emperor were alive today, he'd send the doctor to the lion's den for the insult.

"He's of no particular breed," the doctor said unnecessarily. "For a while he used to give me a lot of trouble eating everything in sight. But that was when he was a puppy. He is getting on in age now and he sleeps most of the day away."

Caesar raised its head for a second as if he knew we were talking about him. Almost as if his head was too heavy to hold up for long, he yawned widely and a great bacon strip of a tongue lolled from his mouth. I could imagine my hand disappearing in one bite, but he dropped his head back onto his paws with a humph and shut his eyes.

"Nice dog," I lied, hoping the gods wouldn't smite me down. "If you don't mind, would you go over everything that happened today?"

He took a breath and glanced out the window, gathering his thoughts.

"Well, it was just like any other day. He likes a walk late in the morning and when I can, I take the leash off and let him run. He likes to do that. When I whistle he comes back, only this time he didn't."

The doctor was talking slowly and haltingly as if putting the sentences together was difficult for him. As he spoke, Caesar sat between us, staring up at me with nearly human intelligence. Sometimes he panted with what looked almost like a grin, tongue dangling. Only his eyes shifted as the doctor spoke, gauging our tones, and no matter how innocent he looked, I had no doubt he would intervene if he didn't like what he heard.

"I whistled again thinking he must have gone a little further than usual and he came running back with the bone in his mouth. At first, I thought he had a stick and wanted me to throw it to him but as he got closer I saw the shape and knew what it was. I took it off him." He smiled as he looked down at the dog. "I had a bit of a fight with him and then I called you people after I was sure of what it was."

And there you have it. *You people.* As if we were another species. As if they belonged to a club and we were only allowed into it from time to time to view the horrors of their world.

"Doctor, do you mind putting the dog back on a leash and taking us to where he brought the bone back to you?"

"No. No. Not at all. I will get the leash."

He stood and made his way through a door to his right, leaving the constable, Sam and me alone with the dog. Caesar slowly rose as the doctor left the room and as quiet as a sentinel, lumbered towards me, head down.

This may be the time to tell you that dogs and I just don't get along. Most of the time, they wet on my shoes or wrap themselves around my leg in a strange mating dance. Caesar approached me and instantly began to smell my crotch. I pushed his head away with my hand and said "Shoo" to him softly and give him his due, he thought about it for a second. He eyed me silently through hooded eyes then walked over to Sam and sat down in front of her.

Sam looked down at the dog and said in a firm voice, emphasising each syllable slowly, "GO. A. WAY," at which he immediately stood up and walked towards the desk and lay down again, his head on his paws.

I stared at her and said, "I'm impressed. Why didn't it do that when *I* spoke to it?"

"Dogs sense tones in voices." She shrugged. "He knew I meant business."

"Hell", the patrolman mumbled from behind me, "I almost took a step back myself until I realised she was talking to the dog."

Sam spun around, about to say something to the patrolman, when the doctor's entrance stopped her short of her reply. I'd seen the look in her eyes and I knew the patrolman had missed out on a Sophia Loren tirade.

"Here we go." Germain jiggled the leash at the dog and Caesar sprang to attention as if he'd been shot out of a rubber band. He issued a high-pitched yelp and squirmed as the doctor connected the leash to the dog's collar.

"Merci beaucoup, le docteur. Après vous," I said with a sweep of my hand towards the door.

Sam came up beside me as the doctor and Caesar led the way up the path to the gates at the entrance. "French, Jack?" she smirked. "You're full of surprises."

"Got to keep some mystery in my repertoire," I said as I wiggled my eyebrows, Groucho Marx style. "Otherwise you'll stop loving me."

3

The overhead canopy of trees blocked out most of the light and provided a slight relief from the hot sun. Circling in the sky was a hawk, its wingspan stretched out as gracefully as a soaring kite.

After sending the patrolman back to the station, I took my coat off, noting that the shoes I was wearing were totally unsuitable for this kind of tracking through the undergrowth. Sam had been smart. In the boot of her car, she produced a pair of runners and a crime scene kit containing a flashlight, a camera and crime tape and I silently wished I'd remembered to put my own kit in the car before heading out that morning.

Within minutes, sweat was running down the side of my face as we made our way through the brush. The insects went nuts as they smelled our flesh and Sam began slapping the back of her legs and neck so much that pretty soon I couldn't tell which red welts were from the bloodsuckers or which were from her hands.

For a while, I tried the Zen trick of ignoring them but after a few hundred bites or so, I gave up. Confucius never had to live in 90% humidity on a 30-degree centigrade day. If he had, he'd have felt like I did and would have decided to hack off a few heads.

Pine needles crunched under my shoes and I struggled for purchase as I trudged behind the doctor and the dog with Sam coming up the rear, like we were part of a straggly entourage. My hands were beginning to get sappy from grabbing hold of trees to keep myself upright.

But if there was any place to escape the heat, we had found it. We were in the shade and a light breeze swirled around us. If I wasn't preternaturally opposed to biting insects, snakes, heat, stinging nettles and dirt, I might have enjoyed the rumoured serenity of the eucalyptus forest.

Ten minutes later, the ground levelled off slightly and the trees thinned.

"This is about where I let him go," Germain called to me over his shoulder.

"Okay, doctor. Release the hound."

I heard a muffled "Oh boy," from Sam but I ignored her.

I heard her slap another mosquito as the dog sprang off in a weaving pattern towards a bank of trees, moving in long steady paces instead of running full bore. Sniffing the breeze, Caesar stopped every now and then, sometimes doubling back a short distance but always moving forward. Germain encouraged him and he sprang off well ahead of us. In the distance, we could hear him thrashing around in the undergrowth. The ground had levelled off even more and subconsciously, I thought that if someone were going to bury a body, it would be done on as even as ground as possible.

As I followed, I began to think that this search could very well be fruitless. As I lost another pint of blood to the mosquitoes, Caesar began zigzagging more erratically through the trees, obviously pleased to be out again but not giving any indication that he was close to finding the spot where he'd found the bone.

Hearing stories from dog handlers, I had an idea that the dog's nose should be on the ground not up in the air most of the time like Caesar's nose seemed to be. That and the fact that he wasn't baying as I'd expected made me think we were wasting our time.

As if reading my thoughts from metres away, Caesar began barking at a spot where the earth had been overturned and as we neared, I could see twigs scattered around.

On closer inspection, they weren't twigs at all.

I dropped to one knee and saw the contracted fingers of a small skeletal hand. Above it was a small skull with a visible crack across the top where soil had lodged.

I have not become used to seeing dead bodies. I felt an invisible punch in my chest as I stared. I knew that no matter how much I tried or how much I wanted it, I could not take evil out of the world. This is the one true thing I know in my life and it's not something you want to consider. Unlike the saying that says, *'The truth will set you free'*, this truth certainly did not. This truth did not allow me to rise above it. It held me down like chains and it weighed heavy in my heart. My life's mission was to go to places where this evil existed and all I could hope for was that it didn't drag me down into its depths as I fought the ugliness. Thirteen years and countless cases and still the horror etched deep grooves in my heart.

I believe people slip-slide into evil. They cross the line for just one moment. Then they cross back. They feel safe but the line is still there. It's still intact. Okay, maybe there's a smudge there now, but they can still see it clearly. And next time they cross, maybe that line smudges a little more. But they have their bearings now. No matter what happens to that line, they remember where it is. At least I hope so.

I could hear leaves rustling and the sound of Sam's feet walking towards me from behind, dry leaves crunching under them. She stopped and let out a tiny puff of air as she whispered, "Oh God, Jack."

I heard sadness in her voice and when I looked up into her eyes, as mosquitoes buzzed around us, my heart pounded heavily in my chest. She grasped the back of her thick hair with one hand and twisted it into a makeshift ponytail as she squinted down at the grave. I knew what she was thinking because every cop goes through it. You wade through the cesspool every day and soon you begin to believe there isn't anything else.

It's surprising the tiny things that you become aware of when your mind seems stuck in a vortex. As I crouched beside the small skeleton, I became aware of thousands of tiny sandflies hovering around me like a grey cloud. A few leaves fell from a nearby eucalyptus tree. A gust of wind rippled across the grass, rolling through it like the muscles of an animal might ripple.

Germain was holding Caesar by the collar and telling him to sit as the dog shifted on his front paws like a kid that needs to go to the toilet. Caesar obeyed and sat panting.

"It looks like a small skeleton from here." The doctor's voice echoed slightly as he called out to me.

"Yes, it is, doctor," I turned and called back to him. "But I don't want you to come over here. The less disruption to the crime scene the better."

I moved a little more of the dirt away with the back of my hand and the rib cage became visible.

I'm going to get who did this, I thought.

I almost said the words out loud. Instead, I cleared my throat and turned to Sam.

"I don't think we need to be concerned about the crime scene being recent, Sam. I'm no anthropologist but this skeleton looks like it could have been here for a long time. And it's definitely a child. We'll still need to seal this area off until the medical examiner can get here." I glanced up at the trees. "Do you have a signal on your mobile?"

Sam pulled her phone out of her pocket and checked the reception bars. "No. No reception at all."

"I didn't think so. You head back to the car and radio this in while I stay here and tape the area up. Take the doctor and the dog with you. I'll meet you back at the house in a bit."

Sam nodded as she tossed the crime scene kit to me and headed off without an argument.

I went to work with the yellow tape tying a length of it around a tree and joining it to others until I had a boundary around the gravesite. As I finished, I took a cursory look around the area.

Something didn't seem right. I was in the middle of a slight clearing, sure, but it was as if the gravesite was in the middle of a much larger cleared area, almost as if it was the bullseye, and the soil contrasted slightly with other nearby soil. It appeared to be less compact. There were more rocks and pebbles around it and the plants that were growing over it were a lot smaller and less sturdy. I couldn't put my finger on what exactly was bothering me, just that the area seemed different somehow.

There wasn't much more I could do except make my way back up the incline.

By now you will have realised I'm not an athlete. The soft ground suddenly gave way under my feet and I stumbled backwards, falling awkwardly as losing my balance. Whether it was fortunate or not, a tree trunk stopped my fall as my midsection slammed sharply against it. I let out a pained "phuff", groaning out loud as I pulled myself upright.

Ten minutes later as I walked into the front yard, both Germain and Sam looked up at me in shock. I looked down at the front of my shirt and saw dirt, grass stains and blood.

"Oh my God," Sam yelped. "What happened?"

"I fell," I said lamely.

"Come here, monsieur," Germain said. "Let me look at your chest."

I shook my head and warded him off with my hands. "No. No. I'm fine. There are just a few scratches, that's all."

I had no want for them to see my chest. Despite my keenness to create an image of 'the new me' while on leave, I wasn't as enthusiastic to gain a suntan to go along with it. Sun tanning has to be the most boring pastime on the planet so at this moment, I am a faint orange, having applied a primer coat of 'Tan in a Can' to disguise my policeman's pallor. What Sam didn't know, and would never see, was I'd missed a few places. My ankles and behind my knees were now ochre and oddly blotched with what looked like hepatitis.

To change the subject, I turned to Sam and asked, "Did you get in touch with the medical examiner?"

She nodded absently, her eyes glued to the blood on my shirt. "They'll be here soon. Jack, let the doctor look at you. Don't be a hero again."

I gave her a pointed look and she had the grace to drop her eyes.

"She's right, you know," Germain said eyeing off my shirt. "The way you're holding yourself as you walk, you've damaged a rib. Maybe broken one. You may have done some other damage as well."

Sam squeezed but I shook my head more vehemently. The last thing I needed was someone telling me I'd broken a rib on my first day back on the job after eight weeks absence. They'd only send me off on another two weeks leave while I watched the next-door neighbour's sprinklers spin and my rib healed.

"Even if I have damaged a rib, there's nothing you can do for it. Right?"

Germain did a so-so action with his head. "But it should perhaps be wrapped."

"Anyway, I've just broken the skin around an old wound. That's all."

Sam's eyes widened even more as I mentioned 'old wound' and I put my hands out in a 'calm down' gesture.

"I'll change my shirt before the rest of the team arrives," I said moving towards the boot of my car and Sam followed, her heels making clopping noises like a horse behind me.

"Are you going to watch me undress?" I asked over my shoulder as I began to unbutton my shirt.

"I want to see the damage."

"Sam, I'm fine. Believe me. It's just a few scratches. Nothing more, I promise."

She walked around to stand in front of me as I unbuttoned my shirt.

I stopped working on the buttons and raised my eyebrows at her. "This is getting close to sexual harassment, Sam."

"Tell me the truth, Jack. Are you sure you're okay?"

I sighed. "I'm sure. Now why don't you take the doctor's statement while we wait for the medical examiner to get here."

It was an order rather than a request because I didn't want to take my shirt off in front of her. Not just because of the colour of my skin, but I could feel my blood drying on the shirt and I knew when I took it off, it would take the top of the already forming scab and it would begin bleeding again. It wouldn't do Sam any good knowing that I'd missed doing some real damage by the width of a tally-ho paper.

4

I became the overseer to the small army that arrived, ready to begin work on the crime scene. The medical examiner was Mary O'Brien, a petite blonde who is way too attractive for such a ghoulish job.

Her eyes twinkled as she closed her car door and walked over to me. "Hey! Look at you! Don't you look super?"

"What?" I asked as I looked down at my 5-year-old suit, seeing dust and grass stains on the knees of the trousers. I pulled a body-builder pose, flexing my muscles, and she grinned as she squeezed a bicep.

"You've lost weight and you're a little toned and buffed which means you're tired of the bachelor life and are seeking out the fairer sex." Her eyebrows went up and down a few times.

At this point, I should say I am no Arnold Schwarzenegger. To tell the truth, before the accident, I had a body that was tending towards cuddly and my pallor was so pale it was as if someone had lifted a rock and found me stuck to the underside, damp and sickly. But in the last eight weeks, I've dropped a little weight and the love handles have smoothed out a little bit.

To relieve the boredom in my convalescence, I took up a sort of jogging which seems to satisfy my masochistic streak. It hurts and I'm slow, so don't get me wrong. I'm not one of these dedicated spandex and

Nike-clad joggers who pound the paths shying away from unsavoury types or even embarrassing ones. I choose a baggy sweat suit that hides my body rather than accentuates it and most of the other joggers look a lot better than I do, believe me. I don't want to look like a condom crammed with peanuts but at my last medical, the doctor told me I was losing my contours and I had to admit, he had a point. As the years progress, it gets harder to stop the weight from going on but nothing that a bullet to the stomach won't fix.

"How was your time off?" Mary asked bringing me out of my reverie.

"Oh, you know. Sex and drugs gets a bit tiresome after a while. Pretty soon you want something more meaningful and fulfilling in your life."

"You picked the wrong day then," she said as she patted me on the arm before walking over to join her crew. I heard her mutter, "Sweet Jesus," as she squatted down beside the skeleton.

Mary's reaction did not surprise me. Most M.E.'s stayed clinical and detached. Not Mary. People were not tissue and messy chemicals to her. I've seen her almost cry over bodies plenty of times and she handled John and Jane Does with incredible respect. I'd even seen her perform autopsies as though she was trying to make the person recover.

The bones came of the ground easily as if they had waited impatiently for many years. Like a team of archaeologists, the team painstakingly used small tools and brushes and work progressed at a fast rate because of the soft soil.

At 4 o'clock, the crew broke for a coffee break and almost the complete skeleton had been recovered and photographed. As well, deteriorated pieces of clothing had also been recovered. Small boxes with rope handles containing the bones had been transported to the forensic pathologist's office and Sam had taken the clothing, most of it unrecognisable, to the crime lab for the same intense scrutiny. Looking at the scraps, I doubted they'd be of any use in identification of the body.

Sam stayed watching by the gravesite as Mary walked over to me with two cups of coffee she'd poured from a thermos. She handed me one and said, "Back one day and look what you go and do to me. I'd call you the Grim Reaper only I think you'd believe me and take offence."

I swallowed a mouthful of the sweet coffee. "Well, I've got to agree with you. I could have done with a quieter start."

"You know, we're not going to find all of the bones," she said. "We won't even come close. We're going to reach a point when the light is too bad for us to continue and even if we do go on, we won't find too much more."

She took a sip of her own coffee. "I want you to keep in mind the depth of the grave and the terrain. They're going to play a key role somehow in finding out who this child is and what happened to him."

"Him? You know it's a boy?" I asked.

She nodded. "By the hip spacing and the underwear. Decomposition fluids helped to destroy the clothing but the waistband was pretty much intact and it's the type used in underwear for males. We're dealing with the bones of a child of about ten years of age with fractures on several parts of the skeleton. I can't confirm that they caused the death of the child, but it's enough evidence for me to say that the body was buried before the fractures had been treated."

"Okay," I nodded. "What about the grave depth."

"The hip assembly and spinal column were undisturbed when we uncovered them. Going on that alone, the grave wasn't any more than a foot deep. A grave that shallow indicates panic and poor planning. But," she held up a finger, "the location being so remote and difficult to access would indicate the opposite. The area seems to have been chosen because it's so hard to get to yet the burial was done in a hurry. This child was barely covered with pine needles and topsoil. We're sending everything to the lab but, to be honest, we don't expect much."

She took another sip of coffee and looked around. "We're in the open here and it's been maybe ten years since he was buried. It's been a long time. I know that pointing this out to you isn't going to help you catch this guy but I think you should know what I'm seeing. One more thing, I don't think you should expect that all of the bones will be here. If that dog brought back an arm, how many other animals have found other bones?"

"Did you have a chance to look around past the gravesite?" I asked. "The area seems more cleared than it should be. I can't put my finger on it but it just doesn't look right to me."

"I can't just bring out the shovels and dig, Jack. First we have to systematically survey the outer area and set up a grid system. I won't have a chance to do much more than I've already done today but I'll be back to finish up tomorrow and I'll do some sampling around the site then."

I asked the question that had been working its way to the surface.

"Are there more bodies here, do you think?"

"I don't know at this stage and there's no indication of that at all. But I *will* make sure. I'll do some sampling and sink some gas probes tomorrow. All purely routine."

I nodded and muttered my thanks. Heading off home seemed the only thing left so I decided to leave and get an early start in the morning. I told Sam we'd be finishing up for the day and we both made our way to our cars, ready to head home and meet back at the site the next morning. Before heading home, I decided to drop off my notes at the station so Pete Bridgman, a junior detective whose job it was to fill in the information board, could have it ready when I gave my brief to the team in the morning.

I wasn't looking forward to tomorrow and the possibilities of multiple victims.

5

It was almost 5 pm and traffic was starting to build on the way back through Surfers Paradise. The sky was a haze of leftover smoke and exhaust fumes. Cars, trucks and buses stretched ahead as far as I could see, moving forward when the traffic lights changed, then coming to a halt again while more traffic flowed across the innumerable intersections.

Fifty delightful minutes later, I turned into my street. The neon lights of my local restaurant flashed up ahead and I half-heartedly thought about stopping to pick up something more substantial to eat.

The place seemed to change nationalities every few months. Last month it was Italian, this month it was Greek with turd-like lumps wrapped in leaves. I'd seen things like that in roadside parks and had never had an urge to put one in my mouth washed down with a beer. Not that I'm partial to those brown-bread-and-sprout restaurants that all look the same: natural varnished wood, healthy hanging plants in macramé baskets and waiters who don't smoke cigarettes but would probably toke on anything else. Deciding not to risk it, I kept going until I reached a drive-through Liquourland store and pulled in to buy a six-pack of VB and crisps before heading home.

I pulled into my driveway and saw day-old junk mail overflowing from the letterbox. I tugged them through the opening, not bothering to unlock and relock the metal flap, then tossed everything except the bills in the garbage bin at the side of the house before letting myself in through the front door. Behind me, a man on a pushbike whizzed by dressed in dark clothes, the heels of his cycle shoes marked with strips of reflector tape. He made no sound except for the soft hum of air through his spokes.

I had forgotten to put the air-conditioning on before I left this morning so there was no welcoming rush of cool air as I opened the front door. Built-up heat washed over me as I tossed my keys onto the small dining table.

The house felt empty. Foreign. The place I called home for a year felt stale and lonely, like the 'before' picture in a magazine. Functional is a good word for my house. So is characterless.

There was a lounge suite, a stereo in a cabinet in the corner and a pile of CDs stacked next to it. A bookshelf stacked with books in a corner overlooked a coffee table in the centre of the room as well as the dining table. The walls were off-white and almost bare, looking like I was either just moving in or just moving out. It looked too bare, lacking creature comforts and decoration.

I know that some people think I live in a strange world that is impossibly far from normal. I even think sometimes my life is like looking through the wrong end of a telescope with the world a long way away from me, but I've almost become accustomed to the solitude my job creates.

Being single can be confusing. On one hand, you long for the simple comfort of companionship; someone to discuss your day with, someone with whom you can celebrate a windfall or someone to just commiserate with you when you have a cold. On the other hand, once you get used to being alone, you wonder if you can take the aggravation of having someone around all the time, or more to the point, not having things your way. Other people have their own opinions, habits and mannerisms not to mention mood swings, likes and dislikes and attitudes that in no way coincide with the correct ones, namely yours.

On the coffee table sat a framed photo I still keep. It was a photo of my ex-wife and me when we'd first started dating in Hobart. We'd spent the day walking through the Queens Domaine with the sound of seagulls shrieking in our ears. Government House had been almost invisible that day and the Tasman Bridge was shrouded in mist - yet again. In the distance near the antique markets of Salamanca Bay, shoebox-shaped brick houses more than a hundred years old lined the narrow streets opposite the harbour. Beneath the snow-caped mountains in the distance, breakers pounded the walls of the harbour like distant thunder and the ocean was the colour of dull steel because of the dense fog.

Sally had asked someone walking by to take the photo and they'd gladly agreed. In the photo, I had my arm resting gently on Sally's shoulder and she had her arm wrapped around my waist as we both smiled and snuggled together as much against the cold as any emotion we were feeling at the time. Someone had a radio on and Frank Sinatra was singing 'Fly Me to the Moon'. Now, every time I hear that song, I always think of that day and the smile always returns. On that day, it was as though there was no life before *us*. No love, no partners and no past before the day we met.

Yeah, I know.

I there the crisps on the dining table with the keys and draped my coat over the back of a chair as I took my tie off. As I was putting the beer in the fridge, I heard a noise behind me and saw Sherlock pushing himself through the cat door.

"Hi there, buddy," I called out.

Sherlock is a refugee from my local RSPCA. I rescued him after I moved to Surfers thinking that having an animal around would somehow break the silence. A dog needed attention, something that I wasn't able to provide in my occupation but a cat, now that was different.

Like a kitten from central casting, he seemed relaxed and friendly, even laid back, as I stared at him through the bars of his cage. It was only after bringing the tabby home that I found out it was a ruse. It turned out that Sherlock was prone to dipping his paw into glasses of beer and knocking then over, his meow sounds like he's being put through a mincer and he prefers drinking from dripping taps in the bathroom, even the toilet bowl, rather than his dish. He also has a radar for muddy puddles. If he could type, he'd punch out 'ha, ha, ha'. Months ago, I'd happily have done him in if I wasn't sure he'd haunt me with his other eight lives.

Mostly, I'm happy to have him around because he never complains about my irregular working hours. Plus he dislikes people, which I must admit endears him to me. For months after bringing him home, he'd give me his version of a foul look, but my time at home seems to have settled him a little.

He walked across the floor and sat by his bowl. 'Naow.'

I took a half-eaten can of Tuna out of the fridge and emptied it onto a plate before sitting it on the floor beside him.

He sniffed at it, lifted his tail in the air and walked towards the back door, ready to head out again. As human as Sherlock is, there is no use in striking up a conversation with him.

I took one of the cans from the six-pack of beer from the fridge and walked out onto what the real estate agent had optimistically dubbed a 'veranda'. It was the size of a very small bedroom. Four people, maybe five, if they stood still, could stand on it at one time. The only piece of furniture was my old recliner, placed there to catch a bit of a breeze. I collapsed into it and popped the top off my beer at the same time.

Despite the relatively clear air, the stillness made me think the fires weren't over yet. The air is never more still than in those moments before the wind begins to howl again, once more torching the scrub into flames. Maybe the stillness was a warning to us not to get too complacent.

On the other side of my back fence, a lawn sprinklers did a slow wave on my neighbour's recently mowed lawn while on the other side, my neighbour, who was always trying to set me up with her big-boned niece with her 'inner beauty', was watering something red and flowering.

As always, ready to jump into my thoughts, was Sally and Jasmine.

Sally, my ex-wife, left me two years ago, taking our 12-year-old daughter with her. 6th August. Wednesday afternoon. I'd always said that Sally would go far, and she did. As far from me as she could.

I had always believed I was able to read Sally's moods. In the beginning when things were good, it made me happy to be able to read her thoughts but towards the end, the open reflections of pain only made me withdraw from her.

Beware of Beautiful Days

For a while after she left me, trying not to think of where my life was headed was hard. I was on a roller coaster ride downhill until twelve months ago when I woke up one morning with the worst hangover I'd ever had. It was only then that I began to ask myself, *'what the hell am I doing with my life?'* When I couldn't answer my own question, I decided there had to be a change. How I should shape my life and how I should account for my time distracted me for a while but thoughts and memories of Sally and Jasmine always crept back.

The worst thing about a policeman's job is what it does to the ones you love. No matter how hard you try to protect them, you only end up alienating them. Over the space of ten years, I saw the subtle changes in Sally but whether I was too stupid or too busy, they never registered as a danger and apathy is always the result. It's easier to lose yourself in work than to cope with reality. Love takes time, effort and work and given human nature, are any of us capable of change? It's easy to see the faults of others but not so easy to see our own.

Being a cop, you see bad things happening every day and the last thing you want is to bring them home with you. I tried to distance myself from it, to deal with it. It's a natural emotion to draw away from pain and to build an emotional wall around yourself. But while you stop pain from getting in, you also stop yourself from getting out. I learnt *that* lesson too late.

I remember Sally's words when I first applied for the promotion to Sergeant. She said, "If you get that job, you'll be impossible to live with." I remember laughing at the time. I got the job and as Sally well knew, I wasn't laughing much these days. Sally saw it as me shutting *her* out so eventually she did what I did. She shut *me* out and took Jazz with her.

Before you know it, you've been pushed towards a fork in the road. The road divides and you have to make a choice. Some people can't choose so they stand at the fork waiting for a sign that never comes. It's just an excuse to leave things unresolved and pretty soon the road is overgrown and they can't pass anymore. The road's closed. So they're stuck there, at the fork, which is the last place they wanted to be in the first place but now it's too late.

But, like me, most people go down some road or other. Days pass.

Then weeks and then months. The scenery changes and pretty soon you realise that there was no way to find your way back to where the road divided in the first place. There *is* no going back. The only thing to do is to move forward. Forge ahead and make new ground.

For a while, I withdrew and I'll admit it wasn't the smartest thing to do and it almost cost me my daughter. Jazz is at that awkward age. Too old to be cuddled and two young to be an adult. Twelve going on twenty. It took me almost a year to follow them to Surfers Paradise and then another six months to pluck up the courage to call Sally and ask to see Jazz. I tried explaining I'm a cop and I deal with the dregs of humanity on a daily basis but our relationship is a work in progress.

These days, I go home to a lot of echoes. Most of the time, I manage to keep the gargoyles in the closet and I make believe I'm content being alone. My job is safe, I know what to expect of it and I'm happy with who I am, even if no one else is. I hate to admit it, but my personal life is something else entirely.

The sorry fact is I've lost just about all of my social skills, the few I had anyway. I don't know how to behave without a badge in my hand anymore. Where my job is concerned, I know what to do and I do it well without having to grab the headlines on the front page of the papers. It's good to know that I can still mess them up with drop shots when my serve doesn't sizzle anymore. As for my personal life, it's just easier living by myself with Sherlock. I guess I'm still bleeding and I know I probably always will.

Things of the heart never end.

I heard a purring noise beside me and saw Sherlock staring up at me with luminous green eyes. His taste for VB has always endeared him to me so while I sat sipping on the second can, I poured some of the beer onto the decking and he bent his head to lap noisily. When he'd finished, he jumped into my lap, licked a paw and dragged it behind his ear repeatedly. He smelled like a pair of two-week-old socks but I left him there and scratched the spot just above the base of his tail, which made his back end rise up to my face. I pushed it back down again before I had a better whiff of the litter he had been sitting in. He began pushing his claws into my pants leg.

I looked out again at what was a black hole in my back yard. It was so quiet, I could almost hear my wristwatch ticking and my heart beating in one of those rare wells of urban silence that gives the city dweller a sense of peace. I basked in it until a squeal of brakes and furious honking broke the spell.

In the darkness, the cicadas were screaming like loud tinnitus in my ears and the wind had picked up. I could hear the sea, whipped up by the wind that was like a low voice continually whispering in the background. Pieces of litter were floating airborne. House lights were still on but they wouldn't be on for long. Surfers Paradise still glowed a sulphurous orange in the distance and I knew the late shift would have their hands full with drunk kids leaving night-clubs and brawling in the streets. There'd be plenty of sore heads tomorrow. Even as these thoughts crossed my mind, I saw the lights next door switch off and seconds later a few more houses followed.

I took another sip of my beer and found it had turned lukewarm while I'd been reminiscing. Warm beer is popular with Europeans, I know, but so was blood sausage and Steven Segal, neither of which has ever appealed to me. It was time to call it a night anyway. Feeling sorry for myself wasn't helping my disposition.

As I lay in bed staring at the ceiling and listening to night sounds, my mind showed me pictures of a tiny skeleton covered in dirt. It made me wonder yet again if I'd made the right decision in coming back to work so soon. Even at all. But then, what else could I do. Being a cop was all I knew.

Sleep was going to be difficult and nothing can keep you up all night as effectively as calculating what condition you'll be in the next day if you don't fall asleep soon.

The mind, I've found, can be a dark hole you can't climb out of.

6

As I expected, I did not sleep well. I woke often and when I did sleep, it was permeated by dreams where shadows stood silently in the darkness watching me.

When I opened my eyes for the last time, it still felt like night time. The darkness was only just easing away leaving a salmon colour in its wake. I had been floating in that groove between slumber and consciousness: that state where you sometimes stumble and plummet and need to grab the sides of the bed. My bedside clock said it was 5.00 am and by that time, after an hour of being not fully asleep yet not fully awake, I decided to get up.

Even at this time in the morning, the air was warm and I could smell seaweed and salt spray in the dense early morning fog that shrouded everything. In Queensland, fog usually means a clear hot day unlike Tasmania where fog usually only clears a couple of hours before sunset.

As I sipped my coffee on the back veranda, clouds hovered over the eastern horizon as the rising sun began to ascend like an egg yolk. Little by little, the night shifted away and the day began to surface as patches of topaz sky streaked with pink appeared between cloud breaks. Behind me, Surfers Paradise still glowed a sulphurous orange.

Suffused light gradually filled the sky as the sun slowly rose in the distance like liquid fire in the crystal blue skies. With the promise of another beautiful day, prickles of apprehension began to surface from somewhere deep inside with the uncertainty of what we would find at the grave site.

I showered and dressed in my 5-year-old grey suit again despite the itching I knew it would cause in the heat, then glanced at my image in the mirror. The face that stared back at me in the bathroom mirror was tired and pale and I had one of those dull aches behind the eyes when you know you haven't had enough sleep, not to mention a couple of drinks the night before with not enough food in between them. Overnight, dark rings had appeared beneath my eyes and amazingly so had more grey hairs. My hound-dog eyes were grainy and I looked like something that had been dragged from the grave. Excuse the expression.

"Ah. It's finally happened," I said to the mirror. "You're dead."

I made a childish face at the reflection before laying down some dry food and water for Sherlock and picking up my keys to lock the door behind me. By 6.30 am, I was turning off the freeway on my way to the mountains.

At this time of year, this stretch of the M1 was one of the ugliest pieces of land on the coast. Treeless and flat with a brown stubble interrupted only by power lines and streetlights, it looked like all of the goodness had been sucked out of the earth. This morning, there was a slight haze to the north and the west and a thin band of cirrus clouds were forming high over the mountains to my right. It was too early to be hot, but I knew it soon would be.

The freeway lights began to switch off one by one as I drove and I remembered before I first came to Surfers Paradise. I was accustomed to seeing the skies of Hobart bright with a light that only comes from brilliant stars. Surfers Paradise is bright all right, but it comes from streetlights, bars, shops and skyscrapers. I used to joke that it was the absence of stars that made people lose their bearings and morals in life. Now I know better. Some of us can find our way with a single light while others lose their way when the sky is as bright as a neon sign. We all learn to adjust and, given time, we use stars that reside inside us rather than the stars in the sky or constellations.

Man, I'm really something at 6 o'clock in the morning.

As I wound my way up the valley, I knew that work would begin at the gravesite early and I drove with a feeling of ominous inevitability. I knew Mary would have already turned up early with vapour probes and she would be beginning the process of sampling other areas around the gravesite as she'd promised yesterday. I knew she would already have started at the crack of dawn but I wanted to be there when, and if, she found anything.

When I arrived at the crime scene, Mary and her crew had finished unloading their equipment and each member had put on gloves and picked a spot. They were leaning on their probes, each about half an inch thick and bent at a right angle near the handle. Pushing them not too far into the ground, they then pulled them out again before moving a little closer towards the original site. Nearby were two rolls of mesh and supports that would be needed later to sieve for evidence.

I felt like when I was fifteen and taking my first real exam. I sat up very straight in the driver's seat and clenched my hands tightly on the wheel. Every bit of my body felt tight. My spine was like a metal rod and my neck muscles felt strained. My jaw clenched involuntarily.

I forced myself to step out of the car just as a sudden breeze curled out of the shadows. I shrugged my shoulders against it because it felt like a premonition of more horror to come.

Mary gave a little start when she saw me.

"Have you got nothing better to do at this time of a morning than look over my shoulder?" she asked.

"I wanted to be here to see if you turn up something."

"That's not going to be for a couple of hours yet. We've only just started setting up the probes and computers. When, or if, they register something, then we start digging. It's going to be a while and I'd rather do it alone if you don't mind."

"Has the coroner had a chance to look at the skeleton yet?"

If I was lucky, I could spend the waiting time with Walt Mason and be back in plenty of time to see what Mary had found.

"He had started to go over it when I left yesterday afternoon." She looked down at the gold watch on her wrist. "It's almost 7.00. He'll be in the morgue by now if you want to talk to him. You know Walt. He starts early most mornings." She grimaced then shuddered. "He says he finds it restful."

7

I hate morgues. I'd always believed the word 'morgue' came from the French word 'mort' meaning death, but it actually comes from another French word 'morgeur' meaning 'to peer' from the days when bodies were plucked from the Seine and displayed to the relatives of the missing through the grilles of a Paris prison.

They may be cool and clean but it's the mixed odours of blood, alcohol, disinfectant and death permeating the cold air that I hate. Maybe it's the formaldehyde. Maybe it's the blood. But whatever smell it is, it infiltrates everything. It's a mixture of decay and chemicals unique to this world. But then again, maybe the thing I hate most about morgues is the silence that has little to do with the absence of noise. It's a silence that comes from a failed heartbeat, a voice silenced forever and all the senses shut down.

In the compact room, there were overhead microphones, a wall of steel lockers and steel tables complete with a ridge running all the way around. Drain basins were connected to the foot of the tables into which water, blood or any other matter is channelled. Hanging from the ceiling over each table was a large set of scales.

Most people would recognise all of it from TV shows but television rarely offers a glimpse of what lays inside the lockers. Dead people on TV were intact, clean and bloodless. What they don't experience is a glimpse of what lays *inside* the lockers and they don't experience the chill and the smell of offal.

Walt Mason is about 40 years old and balding with an underwater fish-belly complexion from spending most of his life inside the morgue. From a photo I'd seen a while ago, he had been a surfer in his teens. He was as tall as the surfboard he was holding and the smile he flashed at the camera had been dazzling. These days, he looks like a member of a boy band gone to seed.

As I walked into the autopsy room, he was sitting at his desk dressed in green scrubs with a Bacon and Egg McMuffin in one hand and the arm bone of the victim in the other hand. He was totally used to all confrontations with death and the halogen lighting in his subterranean world gave him a greenish tinge as if he too was decaying.

"Has anyone ever told you you're a ghoul?" I asked.

He glanced up with the burger halfway to his mouth. "Well, hello Serpico. Can't keep a good man down, eh, or is just that no one else wants you?"

"Nice to see you, too, Walt," I smiled.

I glanced over to the autopsy table and saw bones spread out across the stainless-steel table. "How are you going with all of this? Have you got anything for me yet?"

He tossed the half-eaten burger onto a greasy wrapper and licked his fingers before wiping them on what looked like a serviette that had already been used several times already.

"While you've been out in the field finding more work for me, I've been doing radiograph work and trying to put this puzzle together," he said.

Walt heaved himself up and stepped over to the stainless-steel table. He looked down at the scattered bones. "As you would have expected, not all of the bones are here. There are pieces missing that would have been taken by animals a long time ago and I've marked the ones I *do* have with tags."

Love, sorrow, laughter and loss all comes down to this, I thought.

Something on a slab. I closed my eyes for a moment, trying to focus. When I opened them, Walt's eyes were raking the small skeleton.

"Bones tell us a lot about how a person lived and died and bones don't lie."

He stopped talking and as I looked at him in the silence, I realised that his eyes looked haunted. After a moment, he took a deep breath and continued in a voice that was full of pity.

"I have to tell you that I've seen a lot of cases but this one blows me away, Jack. This one is bad."

At his words, I braced myself. "Okay. Tell me what you've got." My voice had come out in a whisper, as if I was talking reverently in a church.

He walked over to his desk and picked up a notebook. "Okay, some of this you'll already know but I'll start at the beginning, so I don't leave out anything."

"Fine by me."

"What we have here are the remains of a young Caucasian male and using the usual growth standards, I would put him at about seven or eight. However, this child has been the victim of severe and prolonged physical abuse, which has caused a growth disruption. What you get is a skeleton that looks younger than it probably is. What I'm saying is this boy looked seven or eight but was closer to ten."

Without even being aware of the fact, I realised I had been standing with my arms folded tightly across my chest, bracing myself for what I knew was coming.

"Any idea when he died?" I asked.

"Hard to determine," he answered. "Radiological testing is far from exact. What I'm estimating is this kid has been in the ground for about ten years. I'm comfortable with that."

I unfolded my arms and pulled my notebook and a pen out of my pocket so I could write all this down despite that fact that I knew I'd get a full report on my desk in a day or so. Walt's estimation put the time of death around 2014 and gave me a good basis for missing person's reports.

"What about the cause of death?" I asked.

"Let's get to that last. I want to talk about the extremities and torso so that you guys have an idea of what this boy endured in his short lifetime." His eyes locked on mine for a moment before looking back down at the bones.

I had an idea of what today would bring. From the first moment as I looked at the small body in the overturned soil, I knew that horror would emerge along with his remains. I breathed deeply, producing a sharp pain around my midsection where the wound from yesterday was healing.

"Firstly, we only have about 70% of his bones here but there has been considerable evidence of skeletal trauma and chronic abuse. I don't know how much you know about anthropological findings so I'm going to assume you know very little. The basic fact is that bones heal themselves and through a study of bone regeneration, we can establish a history of abuse. These bones display multiple lesions in varying stages of healing. Some of the fractures are old. A couple are new. In short, this boy spent a good part of his life either healing or being hurt and that's only talking about bones. There's no way of uncovering the amount of damage inflicted on organs and tissue." His eyes held mine. "Or on his mind."

The knuckles of my right hand clutching my pen were white from holding it too tightly. For a cop, it's not always easy to disconnect when you see crime on a daily basis. Every investigation is different, and some are worse than others.

Walt went to the x-ray box on the wall and switched on the light. Clipped to the box were two x-rays of long bones. "These are x-rays of the boy's femurs."

He chewed his bottom lip for a few seconds as his eyes roamed over the x-rays. "As you can see, his right leg was considerably shorter than his left and would have been congenital. He would have had a limp. Sometimes, in instances like this, special shoes are made where one shoe is built up higher to even up the walk. I should imagine this will be a good way of uncovering his identity." He looked over his shoulder at me. "If there was a missing person's report made, that is."

He ran his finger along the stem of the right leg. "These lesions are thin layers of new bone that grow beneath the surface in the area of trauma. This line here," he pointed to the left leg, "where the colour changes, is a recent lesion which means trauma suffered a few weeks before his death. It didn't break the bone, but it damaged it. It would have caused severe bruising and would have affected his walk even more so. What I'm saying is it could not have gone unnoticed."

Walt pointed to the surface of the bones. "What we have here is periosteal shearing on both limbs which means a stripping of the bone's surface when the limb has been struck violently with an instrument. Recovery patterns show that this type of trauma happened often and repeatedly."

He picked up his notes and glanced at them again before walking over to his desk and picking up the humerus that had been resting beside the Egg McMuffin.

"This is a right humerus and shows two separate fractures. One is at the medial epicondyle. The other break is longitudinal which would be the result of twisting the arm with great force." He looked up from the arm. "And it happened more than once."

He put the humerus down and picked up one of the lower bones. "This ulna shows a healed fracture with a slight deviation in the bone."

I stared at him. "What do you mean? It wasn't set?"

"That's exactly what I mean. This is the type of injury that is called a defensive injury. You hold up your arm to ward off an attack and take the blow to the forearm. Because of the lack of medical attention, I would suppose it was part of the abuse pattern."

He placed the bone back on the table and pointed to the ribs. "These ribs show several fractures in various stages of healing, one that was inflicted when he would have been about three years old. In infants, it's indicative of violent shaking. In older children, it would come from a severe blow to the back."

I found I'd been gritting my teeth and holding my breath. To get the blood flowing through my heart again, I took a deep breath. There was a whirring sound in my ears like wind blowing in seashells. My palms felt damp and I could feel a balloon of heat rising from my stomach into my throat. I could feel the rush of blood to my temples and a chill ran down my back. My left hand was opening and closing at my side.

Death can be natural, but I see it most often as a manifestation of evil. Like other cops who see this face of death, we age more rapidly than normal people. The extra years don't show but you feel them deep in your marrow and your heart and they weigh you down.

I shut my notebook with a snap. "Excuse me. I have to wash my face."

I could have sworn the voice coming out of my mouth wasn't mine. It sounded coarse and weak. I walked into the bathroom and headed over to the sink then turned the cold water tap on. Using both my hands, I cupped the water and tossed it in my face and eyes. In the mirror, my face was red and my eyes looked haunted.

You hear about things like this and you read the reports, but I still can't imagine the level of cruelty that a person would carry inside of them to inflict this much pain on another individual, much less a child.

My mother used to tell me there were no monsters in our world, no real ones. They only existed in movies. She was wrong. They're all around us and if we give them the opportunity, they'll crawl out from under their rocks. From experience, I knew this guy wouldn't look like a monster. He'll look very average. He'll have a demeanour that will not provoke suspicion. He'll be the sort of bloke you wouldn't look at twice, and certainly wouldn't suspect of being a monster. He could be the one who laughs too loudly, the one who thinks he's making jokes when he's actually being deeply offensive or the one who sometimes seems to have drifted off in a daydream all of his own. He could be the one who doesn't really have any friends, who will join in with the group but never pair off with one buddy in particular. But despite all this theory, no one knows what a monster actually looks like.

Back in the autopsy room, Walt was waiting for me to return. His eyes held a softness that I'd never seen before in him and somewhere deep inside, I realised that like me, his callousness was merely a detachment from the horror he saw every day and was no different to mine. What I pray for is that my faith is not shaken by the horror or the unfairness of such cruelty, but only makes me stronger and more determined to end what I see as nothing but brutality.

"It's hard to comprehend someone suffering this much, I know," he said as he patted my shoulder.

"So what was the actual cause of death?" I asked, fighting to keep my voice even.

He gave a deep sigh and picked up the tiny skull in one hand. "What we have here is a skull that exhibits two distinct fractures at varying times of healing."

He pointed to a small crack at the base of the skull. "This one is small and healed because the lesions are fused."

He turned the skull over and showed me another fracture. "As you can see, this one behind where his ear would have been, has tiny web-like fissures with no consolidation and would have occurred at the time of death caused by a tremendous blow from a hard object. A pipe...a bat... something like that."

All I could do was stare down at the skull as Walt turned it over again so that the eye sockets looked up at me. "There are other injuries to the head but none fatal. The nose bones show new bone formation following trauma."

Walt returned the skull reverently to the table. "All injuries will be outlined in my report so I don't need to summarise them for you, Jack. But in short, someone beat the shit out of the boy on a regular basis and eventually, they went too far."

He turned to face me. "There is a glimmer of hope for you in catching this animal, though."

"The congenital difference in the leg bones?" I asked.

He nodded. "Exactly. There should be records of that somewhere. It's not something that went unnoticed. It would have been serious enough to be put in a file somewhere. Also, the first skull fracture would have been serious enough to warrant medical attention. The two together in one file would be conclusive evidence of identity."

I felt like the floor was tilting beneath my feet. "When this kid went to the hospital, wouldn't the doctors see what was happening to him? What about teachers and friends?"

"You know the answers to that as well as I do, Jack," Walt said. "Children are reliant on their parents. In abuse situations, they hate their parents as well as loving them and they don't want to lose the little they have and be alone. Sometimes they don't cry out because they think that no one will believe them."

"But the fractures? Surely the doctors saw this," I waved my hands at the x-rays.

"That's the irony of my job. I see tragedy like this all the time but to a doctor ten years ago, it might not have been so apparent especially if the parents had a plausible explanation." We both stared at the x-rays. "The different length of his legs is the best explanation of all." He shrugged. "They would have said he was clumsy."

Walt gathered up his notes. "That's it from the scientific side. You'll get my full report later on in the day."

I could see the muscles rigid with anger beneath his shirt as I looked at him.

He was still pulling his notes together when he said, "On a purely personal level," he glanced up, "I hope you find the monster who did this. He deserves everything you can throw at him. And then some."

"Have no doubt, doctor. I'll find him."

"You know, it doesn't make me believe in a God that could let this happen. It makes me believe in creatures that live somewhere in the bowels of the earth not fit to walk around with the rest of us."

He was right. Being a cop, I know things and see things that most people don't. There's a subtle sixth sense that most experienced investigators have developed over their careers. It's sometimes a scent or a feeling that permeates the crime scene. I have always taken advantage of these thoughts and impressions. Because of my training, it wasn't only kids I watch, it's the people who watch the kids. I used to find myself subconsciously scanning people when the three of us went out and it was a rare day I didn't see someone suspicious. I'd point him out to Jasmine and say, *'Watch out for men who do what he's doing.'* Sally would get upset and say I was scaring our child but Jasmine would watch anyway. He would pretend to be reading a paper but over the top he'd be watching the kids. I told Sally I was educating Jasmine by training her in vigilance. Sally said I went too far, but it wasn't her that got called out in the middle of the night to a crime scene to view the corpse of a young child.

I didn't have anything else to add. What could I say? I already knew this killer was someone I couldn't reason with. A predator almost. Someone whose mind was incapable of normal human emotion. And this would make him dangerous.

I thanked Walt and headed back to Tamborine Mountain.

8

The sun was rising inch by inch, high in the sky, pulling the shadows shorter and shorter. The morning heat shimmered off the roads and cars and gave an illusion of a silver lining. White gulls floated and circled overhead and girls in minuscule bikinis soaked up the sun with no regard for the ads on television about slip, slop and slapping. I turned on the radio and Phil Collins was singing, 'Another Day in Paradise.'

In the heat, the highway looked as if it was tinted a metallic blue under the harsh sun and even with the air-conditioning running on max, I could feel the heat prickle the skin at the nape of my neck.

I stopped for petrol on the way and bought a pack of sandwiches made in the previous calendar year. The shop wasn't air-conditioned, but it was out of the sun. A ceiling fan blowing down over the counter dried my sweat, giving me an illusion of coolness. I forced half of the sandwiches down, the rest I tossed in a bin by the petrol geyser.

Once I was free of the traffic, it took me half an hour up the winding road of the mountain to arrive back at the crime scene. I turned the engine off and the Camry ticked gently as it cooled.

I took in the scene before me. Media vans were stacked up behind roadblocks and reporters had gathered in groups behind police barricades waiting for any notable person to arrive on the scene. A news helicopter circled above the department's helicopter and together with the gaggle of reporters, the noise and the dust they created would have rivalled Hiroshima. Ahead, I saw the flashing lights of at least six patrol cars. Two policemen were stringing more yellow tape around the trees, like a terrible parody of a wedding circle, while a young, baby-faced cop was holding back the gawkers and keeping a wary eye on the reporters. Murder was always big news but on Tamborine Mountain, it was *really* big news.

The heat outside hit me like opening a furnace. Another molten lava summer's day in the sunshine state. It felt like a million degrees in the sun as I walked towards the baby-faced cop and showed him my badge. His mood must have matched mine because he only grunted at me and waved me through with a backwards flick of his hand. He looked fresh out of the academy and for at least a year, all I'd trust him to do was clean his weapon three times a week and polish his badge and shoes every night.

"Is Detective Neil here?" I asked.

He produced a tight smile. "Female? Pretty? Built?"

I had to give Baby Face diplomacy points for leaving out a more colourful description of my partner's attributes. He may not be the brightest bulb on the tree but he had a future as Chief of Police ahead of him with those 'internal relations' skills.

"Sounds about right," I replied.

Baby Face stuck out a finger in the direction of Mary's crew and went back to glaring at the reporters.

I crunched my way over the litter of fallen leaves and nodded to a few people I recognised. A few brightened when they saw me, ready to ask some questions, but I kept walking. A woman with hair as black as a Vogue model muttered something under her breath and by the expression on her face, she wasn't wishing me a good day. Every now and then I got a whiff of an unmistakeable smell, a smell that is sweet and pungent all at once. It was a smell you instantly know the meaning of, even if you've never smelled it before. It's simply a smell that tells you that this is death and decay.

Sam was standing with her arms folded across her chest dressed in white disposable overalls with booties to match, watching Mary's crew. When she saw me, she walked over to meet me. A whiff of something flowery drifted towards me making the contrast between the eucalyptus and decay even more obvious.

I jerked my head towards the wall of reporters. "How the hell did they find out about this?" I asked.

She was shaking her head. "They're vultures and they're circling. Why do they even bother? They know we're not going to tell them anything this early on in the investigation," she muttered, running a hand through her hair. She sounded disgruntled and off balance and her voice sounded flat to my ears. I knew she had news that I wasn't going to like.

I wiped a trickle of sweat off the tip of my nose and blinked against the brassy sun in my eyes.

"People love to hear stories like this, Sam," I said quietly.

She puffed air through her nostrils derisively.

"Muggings, for most people, aren't at all entertaining because it can happen to anybody at anytime," I continued. "But this? This seems so out of the question to ordinary people. It's fascinating because it's so hideous and terrifying that it may as well be fiction. It's like the stories that fill us with a sense of the spectacular and the absolutely terrifying." I glanced over towards the reporters. "They're drooling with anticipation."

A helicopter from one of the news stations flew over us and then made an arc over the motorway heading to the west where a plume of smoke rose over the mountains.

In my peripheral vision, I saw Mary straighten and crab-walk under the crime scene tape, stripping off a pair of latex gloves as she went and shaking the white talcum powder off her skin in one fluid motion. As she walked towards us, she dusted the back of her overalls with one hand while the other brushed a stray strand of hair off her forehead with the back of her wrist. It made her look even more tired than I knew she had to be.

As she walked towards us, she held my gaze. Normally, it was like rising from a deep dive and finding yourself not in the air but in those blue eyes that were the colour of a summer sky. Today, they were cloudy with dark rings circling them. As she came close, I smelt a menthol and camphor compound that reminded me of Vicks Vaporub and I saw a shine on Mary's top lip. I knew what it was. I'd seen it before and it had a dual purpose. While it was a compound she used to help mask the smell, at the same time it opened her nasal passages to stimulate the olfactory cells and kept her smelling the decomposition to a much lesser degree throughout the day, helping her brain connect the good smell from the bad. Without it, sooner or later, your brain receives the message from your olfactory cells that something bad is out there but after it receives the same message again and again, the signal stops registering. For me, once the smell gets in my nostrils, it never seems to leave, not to mention the residual odour on my clothes when I get home.

Reading the body language of both her and Sam, I asked, "You've found more skeletons, haven't you?" Even in the warmth, I felt a chill that went down to my bones. Only yesterday, I was hoping for a big case to get myself back on track again after my time off. Be careful what you wish for.

"Sadly, yes," she nodded.

In her hand was a map with grid lines marked and the position of the graves they'd found. This would be used in court to have a precise record of where the remains and any evidence were found.

"We've found four more bodies so far and they're all on their way to the lab," she stated. "I'd say the one from yesterday was the earliest killing. Forensics are going to have a hell of a time identifying any of them."

She glanced over to her crew all dressed in white coveralls, looking like little gnomes, hunched over, heads down, digging in the soil. The photographer was standing by the gravesite taking photos of the edge of each grave. His job was to catalogue all the physical evidence to help us identify the killer and the photos could help in identifying possible tool marks. Then they tag and bag everything in sight and leave it to the detectives to sort out later.

"Yesterday's body is different from the rest we've found today." Mary pressed her lips tightly together for a second before continuing. "The one yesterday showed a lot of physical trauma. These ones, I'm pleased to say, aren't quite as bad physically, but worse in a different sort of way." She gave me a rueful smile. "The ones we've found today were all bound with rope, just ordinary rope, but there's no evidence of wounds, blows, bleeding, gunshot wounds," she shrugged, "anything. Plus, they were all twisted in very odd positions when they were buried. From what I'm seeing here, I'd say whoever did this tied them up and then buried them. Maybe they were even alive at the time. A couple of them had backpacks buried with them but after years outside, don't expect them to contain a lot of evidence."

Once more, familiar knots tied and untied themselves in my stomach. Two months ago, I would have said that for overall vomit-inducing horror, it's hard to beat the burnt remains of a body. That case involved a woman who died alone in her bed while her house burnt down around her. The smell of burnt flesh never leaves your nostrils. It's in your hair and on your clothes for days. I would have said that after twelve years on the job, there were few things that shocked me more. I would have been wrong.

As horrific as that last case had been, it fades into insignificance when you see the bodies of children mutilated by fellow human beings. It's hard to have faith in your fellow man when you're forced to look at some of his handiwork. Every case is a battle in a war and believe me, you need something to take with you into every fight. Something to hold onto that drives you. An emotional connection. The twisted remains of these children did that for me.

I had the feeling while I was standing there at the gravesite that they were there too, watching, cold and frightened, and they were whispering the name of their attacker. The feeling was haunting my thoughts. I could only imagine the horror those kids had felt as they lay tied and helpless, struggling to breathe. Their minds must have created a frenzy of panic in every neuron, in every cell, that would have gone far beyond terror when the unanticipated was happening.

The scene reminded me of photos I'd seen of Germany at the end of the Second World War. *Defeat* was not a big enough word. Perhaps *Armageddon* was more like it. I'd read somewhere that every time the phone company dug a trench for a cable, they found skulls and bones and bits of china. Every time ground was broken to lay foundations, a priest stood by before the bull dozers took their first bite. *They started it,* our parents used to say about the Germans, but these boys buried before me hadn't started anything.

When my mind travels along these lines, it leads to a logical conclusion: I become too involved. Once my fire has been stoked, I have to be careful not to let the following sea, a huge wave that comes up from behind you, hit me in my blind spot and tip me over.

Mary's voice bought me back to reality.

"There's something else you should be aware of. The first boy was buried in the centre. All the others were buried around that first one." She looked over to the work site then back at me. "And I almost hate to say this, but the circle isn't complete. There may be no significance at all in that fact but I wouldn't count on it. To me, it would seem that the killer has left room for more."

She sighed deeply. "There's another thing that I find strange. The first boy has been here for about ten years. Walt told you that too, didn't he?"

I nodded silently not sure of where she was going.

"Well, the ones we've found today are more recent than that. Much more recent. And some more so than others."

"What are you saying Mary? They weren't all killed at the same time?"

I was having difficulty getting my mind around this. This is the sort of thing that fills a cop with horror. Gang killings, drug killings, killing the wife because she forgot to video the football match – we know how to deal with those because one thing leads to another. But killing children on a regular basis? That was something else. There was no explanation or excuse for that.

Mary was shaking her head. "Nowhere close. The first two today, I'd say have been here between five and seven years. The next one we uncovered has been here about three to four years, and the last one was only about two years old." She took a deep breath. "But with this much odour, I think we'll find another one soon where the remains aren't completely skeletonised yet." Her eyes raked the gravesite. "There's another one here somewhere. A fresher one, maybe only a year old, which is probably what attracted the dog in the first place."

"He was still killing children a year ago?"

She shrugged and then nodded. "From the evidence I'm seeing here today, that's what I'd say."

Inside, I cringed. I knew that seeing a body after a year is more horrible than seeing, well, a fresh one, not to mention it being a child.

A stronger smell of decay wafter over towards us and from a short distance away, a call rang out. "We've got another one here, Mary."

All heads turned towards the voice and even from where I stood, I could see the tiny misshapen figure that was in some places bone, some places hair and some places leathery tissue.

I never can manage to be a cold observer. Perhaps those much-flaunted tricks of divorcing one's mind from the victim's humanity works for some, but not for me and as I glanced at the faces of Mary's team who have seen this sort of thing so often before, I saw that there wasn't coldness there either. There was only a quiet compassion for the terrible things that had happened to these children.

The body was lying face down. The underside, from what I could see, was a gooey mess. This boy had been wearing jeans and runners and like one of the other boys, a backpack had been buried with him. A black t-shirt covered the upper portion of his body but what was visible was part mummy, part skeleton and part waxwork figure. This last aspect was due to adipocere, a soap-like substance produced during one of the phases of decomposition. After a while, body fats convert to fatty acids and areas of the body are covered with what looks like a waxy surface.

Mary looked at me and drew the back of her hand across her forehead again. "And there you have it," she said softly. "Five today so far. Six altogether. But I'll keep at it. You've definitely got a serial killer here, Jack."

There was nothing else we could do here. Mary had work to do and so did Sam and I.

As we walked back to the car, I said, "There's nothing much we can do here. Let's head back to the station."

"Fine by me," she said. "I could do with some air-conditioning."

9

Homicide detectives are a breed amongst themselves. Some see their job as a skill or talent; others see it as a mission in life. Some are motivated by the need to set things right in an imperfect world. I see myself as incorporating all three.

I have also known some detectives who treat their job almost as a game. They have an inner deficit that makes them want to prove they are better and smarter than their quarry. They have this need to validate themselves to the world at large. These people never last long. They run around making a lot of noise without keeping to a fixed schedule.

This morning, the squad room was littered with KFC boxes, empty chip packets and chocolate wrappers. Several detectives were sitting at their computers and Pete Bridgman was talking on the phone behind a desk by a window. He nodded in my direction when he saw me. I glanced at the information board and as usual, he had been in early to prepare it from the notes I'd dropped on his desk late yesterday.

I took my notes from the inside pocket of my jacket and hung it over the back of my chair, glancing at my desk at the same time. A 'While You Were Out' sticker sat near the phone that said *While you were out* 'Mick Jagger called to say he misses you and without you he can't get no satisfaction'. My eyes travelled over the bent heads but no one was paying any special attention to me. I screwed it up and threw it in the bin without a comment before walking over to the water cooler and filling a paper cup with water. I had a lot of talking to do.

Part of my routine is to observe, note, file and calculate. I look for nuances, inflections and subtle distinctions in behaviour patterns. There is a bond between victim and cop that starts at the crime scene. A bond that can't be severed until the crime has been solved, making them a sort of avenging angel. These angels make the best investigators.

This last feature has helped me on numerous occasions over the years. Next, I write everything down. I carry my notebook around with me like a priest carries a bible. Every investigation is different but there are certain shared characteristics, namely the painstaking accumulation of information and the patience required. You hope for things like a chance remark, an ex-spouse with a grudge or sometimes even an item overlooked at the scene of the crime. What you expect are dead ends, bureaucratic bull, trails that go nowhere and denials. As Mel Brooks once said, 'Hope for the best. Expect the worst.' What you know is that you've done all this before and you have the determination to pull it off.

After all that, I try to slot everything into its right place and sit back to think when all the evidence is collected. Time is always the essence in a murder investigation. There is a window of time during which physical evidence is usually found. That window grows smaller every day.

Keeping an up-to-date log of who you interviewed was the most important part of any investigation. If reports lagged behind too much, no one but the interviewing officer knows what was going on and that's when mistakes get made. The facts had to be available to everyone. As Sherlock Holmes once said, you should never theorise before you have the facts because then you twist the facts to suit the theory rather than arriving at theories to suit the facts.

Having said all that, I must admit I am probably the worst offender. While things are fresh in my mind, I like to jump from one interview to the next rather than lose my momentum by heading into the station to type a report. Another significant fact is the amount of time it took me to type out the reports. You couldn't call me computer literate. All that talk about floppy *this* and hard *that* simply sounds lewd to me. I can beat out a report on an old Remington in the time it takes me to find my way around a computer especially when the PC's are always going down on me. Excuse the expression.

No one said a word as they waited for me to continue. Telephones rang, computer keys clicked and policemen stood in the corridors shouting back and forth to each other but in this room, I had everyone's full attention.

Someone's voice from the back of the room said, "Good to see you back again, Jack," followed by a straggly round of clapping.

I stopped and looked around. There wasn't one officer in front of me that I couldn't totally trust and depend on. Sadly, however, there is a turning point in some policemen's career step when they cross the line. Some stay true, others say *'What the heck!'* And there you have it. Policeman encounter certain temptations that some don't seem able to resist. These temptations come to us a teaspoon at a time until a few suddenly discover they made an irrevocable hard left turn somewhere down the road and they have no idea who they are anymore. I've seen it happen.

The euphoria of solving crimes was extraordinary and these policemen and women in front of me had known that high plenty of times. It was a powerful feeling. As for me, it was gratifying to know that *my* job was to shine the light down the right path for them. This time though, I had precious little to help them with.

I cleared my throat. "Thanks, guys, but I wish it were under better circumstances."

I nodded my thanks to Pete and cleared my voice.

"Sam and I were called to a property in the Tamborine Valley area yesterday afternoon where a dog returned from a run with a bone that has since been identified as the humerus of a young boy aged at about ten years old. We then let the dog lead us back to where the rest of the body was buried."

Everyone's eyes were alert and watching me.

"I'm sorry to say that the boy is undoubtedly a homicide victim."

Every cop knows the statutory definition of homicide. It's the *'unlawful killing of one human being by another'*. Sometimes we add the phrase *'with malice'* which is the concept serving to distinguish murder from the numerous other occasions in which people deprive each other of life – wars coming foremost to mind. In law, *'malice'* doesn't necessarily convey hatred but refers instead to a conscious desire to inflict serious injury.

The victims of unsolved murders are the ones who reside in limbo, some sort of state between life and death, restless and longing for release and yet persistent in their desire for vindication. A place such as limbo is a fanciful notion for someone like me who is not generally given to flights of imagination but it's something I've come to believe. I was determined that this case was not going to be one of those.

I cleared my throat again and parked my rear end on the corner of a table.

"We called Mary to the scene and she informed us that the body had been in its grave for quite a few years. Her guess was around ten years, which was later confirmed by the forensic pathologist, Walt Mason. What we also found was disturbance around the area and, at my request, she brought in gas probes this morning to do a more thorough search. As of now, she has uncovered six bodies, all boys, with maybe more to come."

Several heads dropped and I heard a few sharp intakes of breath.

"What I'm about to tell you is going to turn your stomach even more. The first boy suffered a great deal at, and before, the time of death and had been most definitely physically abused for years, probably most of his life. This was no crime of passion. Whoever did this abused him on a regular basis and went too far. It's up to us to find out who and why."

I looked around and saw disbelief and anger reflected in everyone's eyes.

I turned to the information board where the basic breakdown of any murder is pinned. Written in a black whiteboard marker was the medical examiner's name, laboratory reference number and the crime report number. All around the inside of the board were the details of the place where the body was found, along with some grisly pictures. The terrible nature of the crime was not diminished by the poor light that filtered through the trees as the sun set over the mountain. The small skull and tiny skeleton was still visible amongst the pine needles and rainforest debris.

"As you all know, most crimes are a means to an end. Most of them are committed out of passion, greed, revenge or to silence someone. Sometimes all of the above. But this case is different because it seems implausible that any of these motives could exist with children so young. Our job is to find out the reason for this crime and that will hopefully lead us to the criminal."

All eyes were locked on me.

"The first boy died as a result of a fractured skull and several other injuries but the other boys were bound at the wrists and more than likely buried alive. On the surface, because of the difference in the M.O. of the bodies recovered, it would appear we may have two killers - one who killed the first boy and a second who killed the other boys. If that is correct, they had to be linked in some way. Two or three of these boys were most likely runaways because they had a backpack buried with them containing spare clothes and some food."

I turned back to the information board and ran my eyes over it before continuing.

"One thing you need to know is that the first boy was surrounded by the bodies of the other boys in what is almost a complete circle. This would suggest that the second killer knew where the first one was buried and the rest were not coincidences. If we're looking at one killer for all the boys that have been found, then something happened to the killer's mind between the first death and the others and we'll need to find out what that something was."

I let that sink in for a moment before I continued. "What I think we have here is a serial killer."

From the back of the room, Pete said, "Come on, Jack. This isn't the United States! This is Surfers Paradise."

"You're right, Pete. The problem in this country is not serial killers. It's domestic violence. It's workplace homicide. It's two guys going into a bar and one pulls out a knife and stabs the other one. When we talk about serial killers, we are talking about a small number of men, and of course women, who do a lot of damage and we are dealing with someone who will most certainly kill again unless he is caught. I believe it is likely that he has already selected his next victim and is familiarising himself with that victim's movements and lifestyle as we speak."

I looked down at my notes and then back up again. "Many people when they think of a serial killer will think of a glassy-eyed lunatic. Someone who looks the part and acts the part. Actually, the typical serial killer is completely ordinary. He doesn't look like a killer. He looks very average. He also has a demeanour that will not provoke suspicion. He's the sort of bloke you wouldn't look at twice, and certainly wouldn't suspect of being a multiple killer. This one is familiar with the Gold Coast and the hinterland because he chose a spot that was difficult to access and far enough away from the populace not to be discovered too soon. This implies someone who lives and probably works in the area, possibly even Brisbane. I don't think he's a casual visitor."

"You keep saying 'he', Jack," Sam called out. She was clicking her pen in and out as she spoke; a nervous habit she had when something bothered her. "They were just children. Couldn't a woman have committed the crimes? She wouldn't need to be strong to overpower a 10-year old."

I was nodding as she spoke. Why *did* I assume the killer was a man? I suppose, because I *felt* that he certainly was. There's no denying statistical fact. It's men who commit obscene crimes like rape, stranger murder and serial murder. It's an exclusively male pathology: the hunting, the planning, the obsessive rage working out its ritual of violence.

"Okay, Sam," I nodded. "You have a point. I could be wrong. But let me explain why I think it's a man. Firstly, carrying the boys up to the burial spot would have been a major obstacle, even for a man. Perhaps they were alive when they were taken up there, but we have to assume they were restrained beforehand. Secondly, in Hobart, part of my training was in profiling and I'll try to characterise him for you by using guidelines that are current around the world. They don't always work but at the moment, this profiling is all we have."

I took a deep breath more to gather my thoughts into a logical sequence.

"Over 90% of serial killers are white males, usually with a middle-class background. This one is most definitely white because most serial killers don't cross racial divides. Unfortunately, the danger of profiles is that they can cut off lines of enquiry so keep an open mind when we start finding suspects. In any case, this guy will more than likely be of above average intelligence, though I would not expect him to have a university degree. His school record is probably quite patchy, with poor attendance and highly variable marks because he has trouble focusing. More than likely, he has experienced a traumatic childhood with physical abuse in his own background. This emotional and psychological abuse warps people out of shape. Typically, he may have been raised in an unstable family. These children tend to spend much of their time on their own and as a result exhibit cruelty at a young age. Most people outgrow these disabilities and become upstanding human beings. Serial killers who have suffered abuse repeat the same mistakes over the course of their own lives. They can't make the transition to adulthood. They want to feel important and they want to feel special. They crave the sense of power and control but they simply can't achieve it."

I reached over for the Styrofoam cup containing water on my desk and took a sip before continuing.

"He will never feel like he has lived up to his potential or other people's expectations of him. This man exhibits an extraordinary level of control in the commission of his murders, so I would expect him to be capable of holding down a steady job, possibly even one with some degree of responsibility and forward planning. I don't think his job will involve much contact with his fellow human beings, since his relationships with others will be characterised by his dysfunctional nature. His victims are all pre-teen boys, which would suggest that he has a need to dominate and control. I wouldn't be surprised to find him working in a technology-related area, possibly with computers. This is an employment area where people can hold down good jobs without having significant people skills. He probably doesn't get on well with his bosses, being inclined to be insubordinate and argumentative."

While I was speaking, Inspector Grayson slipped into the back of the room and parked his six-foot frame and ample posterior on the edge of a table. I hadn't seen him since my return but he hadn't changed much in the six weeks I'd been away. His acne-pocked face was still as podgy as ever, the bags under his eyes were still there and the shiny head still glowed under the florescent lights while the two grey caterpillars he used as eyebrows still hovered over intelligent eyes that missed nothing.

I feel an ornery kind of kinship with the inspector. He's tough, emotionless, harsh and mean, all with an overriding competence. He knows his business and he takes no guff. Despite the fact he gives me a hard time whenever he can and without sounding like I'm making excuses for myself, he knows my history and grudgingly likes me.

He nodded to me and I nodded back as I continued talking.

"He's the one who laughs too loudly at jokes although he doesn't have any real buddy in particular. He has little insight into his social failings. He prefers to be alone with his fantasies, because when others are involved socially, he can't fully control what's happening around him."

"He is the sort who has a tantrum because his girlfriend has forgotten to buy his favourite cereal and he believes he's absolutely justified. He thinks that in his crimes, all he is doing is actually committing the actions that everybody else wants to do but lacks the initiative for. He has a big chip on his shoulder and feels that the world has conspired against him. How come, since he's so bright and talented, he's not running the company instead of doing this poxy job? How come since he's so charming, he's not going out with some supermodel? The answer to those questions is: the world is out to get him. He has the egocentric view of the spoiled child and has no insight into the impact of his behaviour on others. All he sees is the way events affect him. Once this hits the papers, he will thrive on the publicity as long as it appears to award him the glamour and respect he craves."

I took another sip of water to gather my thoughts. "The way we found the boys, you might say it was the work of a sociopath, right? Someone who knew damn well what he was doing? Your basic low-life criminal trying to fake being crazy because he thinks it'll throw us off his track? Well, you could be right. Either that or he thinks it'll be easier to spend time in an insane institution than a jail. But that sort of thinking makes him sane." I looked around and let that sink in before continuing.

I took a deep breath. "The first thing we need to do is put together a list of things we need to do."

Everyone had pens ready to write and as I spoke, I glanced across at Sam who nodded.

"We need search warrants to find medical records at local hospitals. That's going to take time and I want you all to help Sam out with the search once she gets the warrants organised. There had to have been something on the first boy. The injuries were too severe and were over a long period of time. I'm going to search through the computer for missing person and runaway reports going back ten years but it's going to be hell trying to match these bodies to any reports, considering the deterioration. At the moment, all we have to go on is the first boy's right leg showed malformation. But somehow these kids are all connected. We just have to find out *who* they all are and *how* they connect. We need to ID this first kid and then maybe he'll point us to the others."

I looked at my watch. "That gives us the afternoon to get going on this." I took a deep breath. All eyes were on me and I looked around at the small team of detectives. As usual, Pete was sitting at his desk still looking like a 5-year-old on his first day of school. His trousers were always pressed trousers. His shirt was always clean but his clothes always seemed a little too small for him with his tree trunk legs and broad shoulders.

"Have no doubt, this was no crime of passion. Whoever did this planned it." I took a deep breath. "But for the life of me, I can't imagine why. It's up to us to find that out. As you all know, most crimes are a means to an end. They're committed out of passion, greed, revenge or to silence someone. Sometimes all of the above. Our job is to find out the reason for the crime and that will hopefully lead us to the criminal."

Papers were being gathered together and feet began shuffling, signalling a restlessness for action but I let that sink in before I continued.

Over the noise, I called out, "Liaise with Sam on this. She will let you know what needs to be done." I stood up and said. "Okay everyone. That's it for todayWe'll meet back here again in the morning."

Chairs scraped back to desks again and papers began rustling.

"I'd like to see you in my office for a moment, Jack," Inspector Grayson called out.

He turned nimbly for someone of his size and walked away, heading in the direction of his office with a billow of cigarette smoke following him.

I gave up smoking six months ago but I wouldn't class myself as a non-smoker yet. I still keep the 'dare you' pack in jacket pocket and I like to get down wind of anyone with a cigarette in their hand so I followed meekly in his wake while I sucked up a lungful of smoke.

"Let Mohammed go to the mountain," I whispered across to Sam.

Grayson sat down heavily in his chair and tented his fingers across his round belly as I followed him into his office. I could hear the air-conditioner droning away in the background but it wasn't enough to take away the thick odour of cigarette smoke.

"First off, let me say it's good to have you back." His voice was deep and husky, weeks away from throat cancer. I nodded and he continued. "Now. This case at Tamborine Mountain, Jack. They're the hardest to solve."

"They are." I had an idea where this was going but I wasn't about to make it easy for him.

"You know as well as I do that the first 48 hours is when people who are going to be caught are caught. That's when the killer is still going to be covered in blood, disposing of clothes and covering his tracks. If witnesses are going to come forward, they already have. I don't have to tell you after those first two days, it gets real hard. But ten years?"

He leant back in his chair and steepled his fingers over his chest. "This is going to use up valuable manpower and drain the budget!" he continued as I stared silently at him.

One of the worst disadvantages about answering to a man like Inspector Grayson, who firstly couldn't say good morning without putting an exclamation point at the end of the sentence and providing an analysis for it, and second.... Don't get me started. With Grayson, I could work my way through to ten with plenty to spare. He was like a dog patrolling his boundaries, barking at anyone who came too close.

"Do you know how many runaways there are?" he asked.

"A lot," I nodded resignedly. "I know."

"There are thousands in Queensland alone."

"I know," I repeated.

"And those are the ones we know are missing but can't find! The ones someone *wants* to find. What about the ones no one cares too much about? What about the ones who have just drifted off and nobody gives a stuff about or has been reported lost? And what about the street kids?"

"My confidence is slipping here," I said.

His eyes looked hard as he replied. "That's not a priority at the moment, Jack. Keeping you confident."

"What do you want me to do?" I asked coolly. "Cover up the bones and pretend they're not there? Tell the old guy to keep his dog on a leash?" I shrugged. "What?"

He stood up and began pacing the room running both hands across his bald head. He didn't look happy, but then again, he seldom did. Veins stood out on his forehead.

"Two words come to mind, Jack. Paperwork and budget! You write the reports and I try to get money to follow them up. This isn't going to be easy to fund so don't start that big brain of yours making any more out of this!"

When I first arrived at Surfers Paradise, I'd heard that Grayson had high blood pressure and he lived in constant fear of a stroke that had killed his father. Mouth to mouth was something I had no wish to perform on him.

"What do you want me to do?" I repeated quietly and pointed to his chair.

Thankfully, he sighed heavily and sank back down in it. He sucked on the inside of his cheek for a few seconds, his two caterpillars working up and down in unison.

"What do you think you've got here?" His voice had calmed and his face had lost the ruddy glow of only a few seconds ago.

I hesitated. There wasn't a lot I could say so I said, "At this early stage, I don't want to sound stupid." I had this paranoid feeling that he thought I wasn't up to the investigation after such a long time away from the job. Paranoia can help to give you an edge and sometimes an edge makes all the difference. "I think we've got a serial killer who has learned enormous self control and who isn't finished yet and I also think he has supreme confidence that he is smarter and cagier than any of us. He is not planning for the day he will be caught. He thinks he's too clever for that and has been very careful to erase forensic traces."

"Save the analysis for the gang out there," he jerked his thumb in the direction of the squad room.

"Hear me out," I said. "Once he finds out that we've found the bodies of these kids, he is almost certainly going to keep a close eye on the investigation, and he will doubtless be laughing his socks off as we run around trying to find him. He's still out there living in the shadows until the next time he kills. And he *will* kill again. Trust my judgement on that one."

"Okay," he nodded. "All I can spare you is three others working the case, you choose which ones, and then I'll only give you a couple of days. No more!" he said. "After that, you move on to stuff that I can justify the manpower for."

I have always been a cynic but at this point, I felt hopelessly out of my league. Principles seemed to be disappearing and I felt like a man who wakes alone on a deserted island to find that all the boats had been stolen during the night. I felt like I was speaking English and everyone else was talking another language. I have always been a loner but at this point, I had never felt more alone. My world was changing and I didn't want it to.

I blinked a few times. "A couple of days?" I said staring at him open-mouthed. "I think you've got me mixed up with someone else. A British guy. Drives an Aston Martin. Goes by the name of Bond. James Bond."

I said it with a massive amount of sarcasm and I saw it put colour into his cheeks. The colour of anger. This kind of reaction can only mean the lid is closing on a boiling pot. We eyeballed each other for a few moments while my good angel and bad angel jostled for possession of my soul. My bad angel said he was a pompous snob who needed to be taught a lesson while my good angel reminded me that my usual vile behaviour had brought me 'naught but grief' and that you catch more flies with honey than you do with vinegar. That was all well and good but hell, he started it and I'm sorry to say my bad angel won.

He took a deep breath and emptied another cigarette out of a bent packet and lit it up, breathing deeply. The colour subsided and his mouth stretched into a semblance of a smile.

"I've missed that humour of yours, Jack." He puffed out a think blue puff of smoke. "But that's the best I can do for you."

"There's six kids buried up there! I haven't even got the reports of the last five yet!"

He punched the stub of his cigarette out in the cup already resembling a volcano. "Don't tell me that because it's just going to piss me off even more!"

He pulled some files towards him and picked up a pen and pointed it at me. "I want something concrete by this time tomorrow that I can pass on up the line. Now get out of here! I've got a lot of work to do here and I can change from being this nice guy sitting before you to someone quite nasty. So let's hope you get something conclusive with those results when they *do* come in because ten-year-old cases come way down the bottom of the list when it comes to recent ones!"

I walked back to my desk and scattered a few things around angrily.

Sam spun her chair around to face me. "He's just doing his job," she said. "It can't be easy."

I straightened up and stared at her. "Et tu, Sam?"

She held her smile. Strangely enough, Sam really liked Grayson and I could never understand that. In return, Grayson always had a nice word for Sam. Sam claimed to see something there besides the lashing-out psychosis that was all *I* ever saw. I once joked with her that she must have pulled out a thorn from his paw at some time.

"How're you going with the warrants?" I asked.

"Just waiting for the emails to come through. Once they do, I'll start phoning around the local hospitals. If something turns up at any of them, I'll head over and see what they've got. What about you?"

"I'm off to the Archives Department to start checking out missing person reports for the past ten years. Since you're so sympathetic with Grayson's plight, you can pick the other two members of the team and get them going with you on this. Pete might be a good one to include. If you need me, you know where to find me."

Half an hour later, I had my list and headed down into the bowels of the earth

10

The basement of Surfers Paradise Police Station serves as the archives department for every case where a report has been made. Up until the mid-nineties, all reports were kept in files and then transferred to microfiche for permanent storage. We now use computers but the process of transferring old data to computer is slow and so far, had only reached the mid-nineties. That meant if I wanted any information for ten years ago, I had to go to archives.

It was nearing 1.00 pm when I arrived and two female clerks were making signs of heading for lunch. The blonde one with the basement pallor and buckteeth looked up at me with surprise as I walked in. I gave her my best smile, my Mel Gibson, and started to speak.

"Good afternoon. I'd like to know if......."

"Forget it, detective," she said before I could say another word. She pointed to a sign on the door. **Closed between 1.00 pm and 2.00 pm.**

"Hey, you give me a hand here and I'll be happy to sit by myself until you both get back from lunch."

"What I suggest is you come back later on this afternoon. I'll be more inclined to be helpful then."

"I don't have until this afternoon." My hound dog eyes implored hers and I could see they were making an impression on her.

"Oh, for goodness sake!" She sighed heavily as her shoulders dropped. "Quickly then. What is it?"

"I need the fiche on missing person reports, 2014 onwards."

"Adult or juvy?"

"Juveniles."

"Okay, well ... good. That cuts it down a lot."

"Thanks." I smiled my dazzler at her again.

"Yeah, right," she said as she rolled her eyes.

She disappeared from the counter and I waited. Three minutes later, she returned with a handful of envelopes containing micro-fiche sheets with the years written on front.

"There's a coffee machine by the entrance," she pointed to a café bar standing beside the door, "if you want something to drink while you go through these."

I thanked her and she left me alone. If the coffee used in this machine was anything like the one in the squad room, it would be relatively tasteless.

Two hours and six coffees later, I had the information I wanted. I handed the list to the one with the death pallor and another fifteen minutes later, I had the files in my hands.

11

When I returned to the squad room, I was the only one in the room, which was what I was hoping for. I needed time alone with the files. There was still a lot of paperwork to be done but I also wanted to step through the evidence and the information slowly so that I didn't miss anything.

I put my jacket over the back of my chair and glanced over towards Sam's desk. The screen saver on her computer gave the impression that you were at warp speed on the Enterprise in a Star Trek episode and headed uncontrollably into a star burst. I gently moved the mouse and the screen cleared to reveal a half-completed report with a note at the bottom that said, *'Do you want to save changes?'* The cursor was patiently blinking. Sam had obviously left in a hurry. Saving everything was a habit as important as breathing to anyone fighting with software on a daily basis. Believe me, I know.

Computers irritate me. When I tell a machine to do something, I don't expect to be asked *'Are you sure you want to do that?'* And how smart can something be when you have to press the start button to shut it down? As a result, I turn my computer on first thing in the morning because it takes its own sweet time booting itself up and I try not to do too much to it until I sit down to do reports at the end of the day.

As I sat down, I saw another 'While you were out' sticker on my desk. *While you were out*, 'the Nobel Prize committee rang to say you were *this* close but PLEASE try again next year.'

I screwed it up and threw it in the bin on top of the other one from this morning.

Minutes later, I had the files scattered all around me on my desk, each file containing a photo, a report of the investigation as well as a newspaper article. Some were turning yellow with age at the edges, and most had notes jotted on the file flaps. Twenty-three files, twenty-three boys.

I felt restless, nearly itchy with the overdose of caffeine running through my system. Now I could feel the stimulants dancing around in my head and I wasn't sure if the emotion I was feeling was due to anxiety or caffeine. Sometimes they both have the same effect.

I tapped my desk with my pen and shifted from my right side to my left as I ploughed through the files. One by one, I read the files but nothing jumped out at me that would connect all of them together. I had a feeling I was missing something that would bridge it all together but I didn't know what that *something* was. I needed one piece of information that would link six of them together and it had to be right here in front of me. But so far, I saw nothing.

From everything I'd learnt about serial killers, they always took something with them. An item of jewellery, a photo, something intimate. Sometimes even a piece of the victim. It gives you an idea of how they see their victims, why they choose one person over another. A trophy is the technical term. But this case was different. There was nothing much to take and no way to know what, if anything, had been taken. Nothing added up.

My stomach growled in protest and I only then realised I'd forgotten lunch. I checked my watch and saw it was 5.00 pm.

When Sam walked in, I was looking down at the photos of the boys on my desk, touching them and squaring them up, arranging them in an abstract way.

"What are you doing here so late?" she asked.

"Apparently like you, I stay late and get in early to impress the boss. Gets you a good reference when you need one. Besides that, I love this place. I can't get enough of these fluorescent lights and the smell of sweat."

She tossed two files on my desk. "Well, I've got some good news for you."

"That's what Brutus said to Caesar," I mumbled.

"Ah, but this time it's for real." She pointed to the files. "We have a positive identification on the first boy. It took all this time for the hospital to dig up the birth records from their archives section but we've got it. A baby named Peter Ashton was born in March 2004 at Southport Hospital to a woman by the name of Angela Ashton, aged sixteen at the time. The father wasn't named on the birth certificate. The child had a slight deformity of his right leg but was otherwise healthy. They took x-rays of the leg and had one taken of his skull as well when he showed swelling around the nasal bridge. The swelling was classed as birth trauma and disappeared a couple of days later. The mother left two days after that. One sheet of paper is all there is to go on and that only contains information such as the mother's address at the time. She was living with her father on an address at the Isle of Capri. I've checked Queensland Transport and a person by the name of Douglas Ashton still lives there."

She propped herself on my desk. "There was a bonus. Their computers also found another report by accident. I asked them for the records of a male child with a deformity of his right leg and these are what we got." She nodded at the files on my desk. "The first one is the birth records of a Peter Ashton. The second one is a report on a 3-year-old brought in with a concussion and a broken arm. He had the same deformity of the right leg. I got pretty excited until I found out the second child's name was Benjamin Preston. Could be the same child and the parents gave a false name to cover up the child abuse or they could be totally different children."

I pulled the two files towards me and opened them. The first one had reports on blood tests and x-rays. The baby had been tiny, almost the size of a doll. The second file was dated 2007 and had handwritten notes from the examining doctor commenting on the deformity and stating the extent of the recent injuries. Two x-rays of the broken arm, one anterior and one lateral, were included in the file along with a skull x-ray which would have been taken because of the possible concussion.

"What do you think? They're one in the same?" I asked.

"Different names but both children having the identical deformity? For a deformity like that, it's pretty rare. Not only that, but Peter Ashton would have been three years old in 2007. That can't be a coincidence."

Sam was right. Sometimes in the case of child abuse, the parents give a false name to cover up the fact that they've taken the same child to the emergency ward with suspicious injuries on other occasions. With a 3-year-old, the name change could very likely go undetected.

"You know what? I think you're right. I'll take these down to Walt Mason before I go home and have him do a comparison with the bones we found just to make sure we're on the right track. Looks good, though. It'll give us somewhere to go on from here. If they are one in the same, we'll go and see Douglas Ashton tomorrow.'

Sam looked down at the files scattered on my desk. "What have you got there?"

"The fruits of my own detection. I spent all afternoon down in Archives. The result is twenty-three files of twenty-three boys between the ages of nine and twelve reported missing in the last ten years. All we have to do now is match six of these files to the bodies of the six found on Tamborine Mountain. There has to be some connection."

Sam was shaking her head as she went from file to file. "You've got to ask yourself, why would kids hitch a ride with a total stranger when they know the dangers? Every kid has it drummed into them from an early age so why would they do it?"

An ambulance went down the esplanade with sirens blaring heading towards Southport and seconds later, a patrol car followed with lights flashing. After the noise faded, I looked at Sam and said, "You think they may have known the person?"

"Like I said, why would they get in the car of a stranger?"

"Okay, what if they felt like they could trust the guy?" I asked.

"That has to be the only answer." A crease was burying itself in her forehead as she concentrated. "So what are the options? What about a neighbour?"

I was shaking my head. "I've gone through all the files. They all lived in different suburbs. A couple lived in Broadbeach, one in Miami, one in Robina and the last one in Mermaid Beach. All within a suburb or two of each other but not close enough to be neighbours."

"School teacher?"

I had my elbows resting on the table, hands clenched with my chin cradled in the hollow. "Don't think so. All of them went to different schools."

"A cop?"

I looked up at her. "Sadly, that's a possibility."

"What about a priest?"

My head did a 'so so' thing before I said, "Not a bad idea." I began flicking from file to file and that's when it hit me.

There are moments in every case when everything alters, just like optical illusions. One minute you're viewing one reality and then, with a tilt of your head, everything changes. Nothing was as it appeared before.

When I was still in primary school, my mother bought me a book of optical illusions. You'd look at, say, palms trees on an island. You'd look a little longer and then, whoosh, it appeared now to be a school of dolphins jumping in the surf. Sometimes, it took a long time and you'd even start to wonder if there was anything different in there at all. And then, suddenly, the image surfaces. That was what was happening now.

The human brain is an amazing organ that no computer can duplicate. It can process zillions of stimuli in a hundredth of a second with a curious mix of chemicals and electrodes. We understand more about the planets and the cosmos than we do about the brain and its workings. And like any tricky compound, we are never sure how it will react to a certain catalyst. That was what was going on now. I was hunched over the desk with the files in front of me as a thought began to process.

I quickly checked a file, then another, separating them into two separate bundles. I couldn't believe I'd missed it before. When I reached the bottom of the pile of files, I had one small pile of five missing boys.

"What's the date today, Sam?" I asked as I stared down at the files.

"2nd January," she smirked. "You've barely been back two days and you can't remember the date?"

I shifted my eyes to her face, *tore* them away from the files. "Have you seen the dates some of these kids went missing?"

I pushed them towards her. "Look." I kept my expression blank but Sam has known me for long enough to read my body language.

She checked one file after another, her eyes widening as they moved from file to file. "Jack?" Her voice was incredulous. "They all disappeared on the 2nd January, only different years.'

She began to shuffle them, placing some in between others, one on top and one on the bottom. She then reached over and picked up the report from Southport Hospital. Her eyes were haunted as they looked back up at me.

"One every year, Jack, dating back to five years ago. The only one missing is the first one, Peter Ashton. He died ten years ago but he's not here."

I'd heard other cops talking about a point in a case where the victim seems to 'reach out' from the grave and points them towards the killer. Once upon a time, I would have thought it was a load of garbage. Just nonsense. As I looked at the files, my reality shifted.

Sam glanced at the door to the squad room and nodded once but the nod seemed strangely out of context, as though her mind was travelling on another wavelength. Her expression didn't change either, which was strange, because she was usually more vocal and more animated than she was at that moment. She just sat there for a while, her eyes wandering from the door to my desk sightlessly. Suddenly, she stood up quickly.

"Oh my God, Jack. There's a…I…I saw…wait a minute," she began stuttering. "I have to…" and then she almost ran out the door.

I sat staring after her blinking stupidly a few times to try to take in what had just happened. I expected some sort of expression of awe, maybe not a Gomer Pyle "Shazam!" but I'd expected something else besides her senseless stuttering.

Two minutes later, Sam walked back into the room accompanied by a fiftyish-looking man. She'd regained her composure and she touched his shoulder as she guided him to a chair on the other side of my desk. "Please take a seat, Mr Caruthers," she said, "This is Sergeant Jack Curtis and he'll be looking after you."

I raised an eyebrow questioningly at Sam and her eyes locked with mine as she spoke. "Sergeant Curtis, Mr Caruthers' son has been missing since this morning."

The room became still, like the lull between songs on a CD. There are moments in your life when it feels like a knife has slashed your skin. One minute, you're going about your work and then it simply unravels. One loose thread and the seam gives way. Despite the fact that my heart had plunged into my stomach and the muscles in my shoulders were bunched, I wrote down the time and name in the log book as if it were any routine investigation. 5.26 pm. 2nd January. Something with a hundred sticky feet crawled along my spine.

Mr Caruthers was wringing his hands nervously but he kept his expression flat as he let his eyes slip off my face to my duty sheet then back up to me again.

"Joey never strays far from home. Never." He rubbed his palm on his forehead and his eyes searched the horizon for words that weren't part of his vocabulary. I noticed his hand had a small quake and I saw his throat swallow. I looked out the window and saw the street lights come on along the esplanade.

Most people who live and work in Surfers Paradise every day take life for granted. When they first arrive, they see the bright lights and tourist traps and even if they close their eyes, the images are still there, imbedded in their mind. But like sunspots, the images eventually begin to fade. They begin to see the flaws. They see the homeless kids going into phone booths and pressing the reject button in the hope they'll find a twenty-cent piece. They see the drunks lying in the parks with empty bottles of cheap booze lying by their side. They see the ten-year olds on pushbikes, one hand on the handle-bars to steer and a can of XXXX in the other hand. And then one day, like me, they see the monsters lurking around the corner waiting, and waiting.

Sam stood looking at me with eyes that had lost their blink reflex.

"He's all I've got now," the old man said. "His mother died two years ago and there's no-one else." His eyes rested in his lap. "He isn't smart. He's what they call 'slow' but we taught him never to talk to strangers so he wouldn't just go off with anyone." His panicked eyes flicked around the room and there was a catch in his voice as he said, "But he's been gone all day."

"Have you tried all of his friends? Maybe someone saw him or knows where he was headed."

Anger flared in his eyes. "Look, you just don't seem to be listening. My son is 10 years old and mentally retarded and he doesn't *have* any friends."

He stared out the window, trying to find the words.

"We had him late in life, you know? A change of life baby they called him. My wife was forty-eight when she fell pregnant and I was fifty-five. Two years ago, my wife died of cancer and since then, it's just been him and me."

He swallowed noisily before he continued and I wrote a note in my notebook. Not because it was important but because I wanted him to know I took him seriously.

"He was always different. We knew it. Everyone knew it. But to look at him, you'd think he was just a normal little boy. Until he starts to talk." The words dried up as his throat closed around his vocal cords.

I stood up and crossed over to the water cooler, filled a paper cup with water and brought it back to the old man. Tears were falling softly down his cheeks and he roughly wiped them away as he stared into his lap. He thanked me and took a sip of water before continuing.

"Kids can be so cruel and hurtful," he continued. "They used to laugh at him when he stuttered and stumbled over words so we sent him to a special school. One that could cater to his needs and everyone was the same."

His eyes raked my face. "He gets scared when his routine changes which is another reason why I'm so worried now. We go together to church, to the shops and he never goes anywhere without me, except to school. He walks the hundred metres there and at three o'clock everyday he walks back home. Occasionally, like this morning, he insists on going to the shop to buy me a paper. He took his backpack with the money and water in it, but he never came home."

He swallowed deeply again, emotion causing his voice to crack again, then he took a deep breath.

Beware of Beautiful Days

"Someone has to believe me. Joey is missing."

12

"I was hoping you'd still be here."

Walt was dressed in his usual scrub greens and standing over a stainless-steel table with one of the tiny skeletons from Tamborine Mountain laying on it. "*Now* what do you want at this time of day? Haven't you given me enough work for one day?"

I placed my briefcase on his desk. Inside were the files but I wanted to see what he had on the five other boys first.

"You're like a dose of the flu," he snarled. "Just when you think you've gotten rid of it, it turns up again."

"Always the cheery word," I grinned.

I'd left Sam and Pete to start the process of processing Joey's missing person's report and I hoped against all hope he wasn't another victim of my serial killer. In my heart, though, I knew. In the meantime, all I could do was to try my hardest to find the killer.

I nodded at the table he was working on. "How are you going? Anything for me yet?"

He glanced up at me. "Translating the technicalities into a layman's language for you," he turned back to the body, "I've autopsied the most recent one in the hope that we'd find something of use but the decomposition was virtually complete and revealed little of significance since all of the soft tissue had collapsed into a greasy mass. Maggots had made hasty work of him. Internal examination confirmed the absence of all organs due to decomposition and there was only a small amount of tissue left representing the gastrointestinal tract, the liver and kidneys. Brain tissue was also completely liquefied. Osseous remains show no evidence."

I put the palm of my hand in the air to stop him as I interrupted. "Pardon? Osseous remains?"

He sighed heavily as he stood back from the table and began to remove the gloves from his hands as he spoke.

"Bony remains showed no evidence of blunt force trauma, no stab wounds that I could see, no gunshot wounds and no crushed or broken bones. There is an old fracture noted but it didn't pertain to his death. I did find ligature marks in the leathery tissue of the wrists which would suggest that his hands had been tied prior to burial."

"All of them were gagged and had their hands tied behind them with rope."

He walked over to his table and tossed the gloves in a basket at one end. "That is correct, my friend. The rope is of no specific type. It's rope that can be bought in any hardware store and can probably be found in every house in Australia."

He picked up some notes from his desk. "The laboratory tests showed no drugs or poisons in his system." He looked up at me. "You may be able to make an identification through dental records because they show care had been taken with his teeth."

He tossed the notes back down on his desk. "Apart from that, there is no way to tell how long the body has been there but a rough estimate can be made from several environmental factors and the extent of the decomposition. My guess is about a year. The others are older and will show even less than this one which is why I autopsied him first. The rest is up to you and the report will be on your desk in due course."

"We think these may be hospital records of the first boy," I said opening up my briefcase and handing him the files. "One file is his birth record, the other file is of an incident that happened to a 3-year-old boy with the same deformity. The ages would have matched. I need you to have a look at the x-rays in both the files and see if they're from the same child."

"The names are different?" he asked, a small frown creasing his forehead.

I nodded. "The names are, but the deformity isn't."

He took them from my outstretched hand and walked to the X-ray light box, clipped the two separate skull x-rays and the leg x-rays onto the glowing screen and stood back. For a long time, he stood silently as he studied them, his head moving from one to the other, then back again. In the light from the light box, his skin glowed a sickly white.

Finally, he said, "The malar and superciliary ridge formation looks similar."

"I'm not an anthropologist, Walt. Tell me in layman's terms, please."

He reached out and drew his finger across the left eyebrow of the baby's x-ray and then down around the outside of the eye. "That's the child's brow ridge and the exterior orbit." He repeated the motion with the 3-year-old's x-ray. "It's wider on the more recent one but that would be in line with his growth."

I nodded slowly, waiting for more.

He picked up the hospital records and began reading the patient history of the 3-year-old. I'd already read the document. The hospital reported the boy was brought into emergency at 3.30 pm on March 11, 2007 by his father who said he found him dazed and unresponsive after falling down a set of stairs. The boy was reported to have had a concussion and broken an arm. The arm was set and six weeks later he returned to the hospital to have the plaster removed. There was no report anywhere in the file of the boy complaining about being mistreated by his father or anyone else. The child was too young for a social worker to see so no follow up had been done.

Walt shook his head while he finished reading the document.

"What?" I asked.

"Nothing. That's the problem. An unsupervised 3-year-old falls down a set of stairs causing major damage and there's no investigation? They just took the father's word? He would have been sitting right there in the room with the child when the examination was done so they just patched the kid up and sent him home again."

"Let's not get too far ahead of ourselves, doc. Let's just I.D. the kid and then we'll go and talk to the father."

"Fine. It's your case but I've seen things like this a hundred times before."

He reached over for a small glass eyepiece and held one end to his eye and the pressed the other against the skull x-ray. He went back and forth several times between the skull x-rays and the leg x-rays, making comparison after comparison. When he finished he straightened up and leaned back against his table.

"I will repeat myself. They should have taken more than one picture of this kid's head. They might have seen some of his other injuries if they had. This child had already suffered by then."

I have come to believe that there is something more than blood and tissue and bone that holds us together. There is something else that keeps us going - something that you will never see on an x-ray. At this young age, this boy had found that *something* to keep himself going despite the abuse he was receiving.

As I stared at the x-rays, I began to believe that his bones had come out of the ground for a reason. They came out for me to do something. And that's what was holding *me* together and kept *me* going. *That* wouldn't show up on an x-ray either.

"Okay. But they didn't do a more thorough examination," was all I could say.

"Yeah, they didn't. But based on what they *did* do and what we've got here, I am able to make several comparison points. There is no doubt in my mind," he gestured towards the glowing light box, "that they are one in the same boy."

"How sure are you?" I asked as he turned the light box off and began collecting the x-rays together.

"Like I said, there's no doubt. It's a match."

"So, if we catch somebody and go into court with this, there aren't going to be any nasty surprises, right?"

Walt looked up at me. "There'll be no surprises. These findings can't be challenged. The only challenge lies in the interpretation of these injuries. I look at this boy and see something horribly wrong. And I will testify to that as well. Gladly. But then you have these official records that state the child was released to his father's care." He gestured dismissively towards the hospital records. "They say he fell down the stairs. That's where the fight will start because I don't think it was as simple as that."

"But there's nothing we can do about it."

"That's the sad part."

He was gathering his papers together. "If you want more on the backpacks, I passed them on to the criminologists." He glanced up at me and raised an eyebrow. "Unlike me, they keep set hours so if you're quick, you may find someone still in the lab. They may have a report by now."

I muttered my thanks and left.

13

The badge on the white lab coat said the man's name was Kevin Wang. The frown on his forehead told me he wasn't pleased to see me. A satchel was hanging over one shoulder and he was in the process of turning the lights off when I stepped into the lab.

"Good afternoon," I glanced at his badge, "Kevin."

He stood frozen, one hand on the door handle and the other on the light switch. His eyes glanced down to the watch on his left wrist and then lifted back to mine. "Can I help you?"

"I know it's late and I'm sorry for that. But I need a minute of your time before you leave for the day."

He sighed heavily. "It's the Tamborine Mountain case, isn't it?"

I nodded. "Have you got anything for me so far?"

"Not much, I'm sorry, but you're welcome to what I have."

His voice was devoid of accent and his white lab coat flapped and swayed as he strode purposefully towards a stainless steel table, dropping the satchel on the floor near a cluttered desk.

I realised this was the only place to rival the autopsy floor in the stench of decay. Scattered over two tables were items of clothing blackened with soil and mould as well as the backpacks.

"We have all six sets of clothes here," he said pointing to both tables. "More specifically, six t-shirts, six pants, six underpants, six sets of socks and six sets of sneakers. The backpacks were the generic type you see in any cheap store all over the country as were the spare clothes inside some of them. No personal identifiers though."

I looked at the collection on the table and then back to Wang. "Anything else?"

He jerked his head in the direction of a door leading out of the lab. "Come with me to the documents lab."

The documents lab contained three desks that were all empty. Each desk had a horizontal lamp, a blotter and a magnifying glass mounted on a pivot. Wang walked over to the middle desk and picked up a plastic evidence bag. Inside was a deteriorated rectangle of paper that had been broken along the fold lines and badly discoloured and decayed.

"This is what happens when stuff gets old and continually wet," Wang said. "It was shoved into the side pocket of one of the backpacks and took us a couple of hours to extract it without doing much damage. As you can see, it came apart in a couple of places. From looking at it under the microscope, we can tell it was a photograph of a woman, but I don't think it'll be much good to you in the way of identification."

He handed the pouch to me and I squinted down at it.

"I can barely *see* it's a woman," I said.

"We'll keep trying to improve the image with some dyes and different lights to bring it up, but like I said, I wouldn't be getting my hopes up about it. The paper is soft and badly deteriorated." He shrugged. "And there you have it. You'll get my report tomorrow."

I thanked him and made my way back to my car. While I'd been inside, a seagull had chosen those moments to deliver a particularly messy parcel on my windscreen and I had to spend the next few minutes clearing it away with a piece of newspaper lying on the back seat before I could head back to the station.

It was almost 7 o'clock as I walked into the station and the lizard part of my brain was telling me it was time to go someplace where they'd put a beer in my hand and give me a steak that hung over both sides of my plate smothered in garlic. Maybe even some pasta to go with it. But first, I had to do a report.

An hour later, the thought of food was too much for me. I'd done a quick version of the day's events and that would have to do. The rest would have to wait for tomorrow.

Five minutes later, I turned off the light on my desk and headed out.

14

The only places open were restaurants, pubs and 24-hour convenience stores, making the traffic light. My usual haunt is King Neptune's but tonight it looked crowded and music throbbed through the front doors. Even if I wanted a seat inside, I doubted they'd have one available. I opted instead for a pub a couple of streets away from Caville Avenue overlooking the ocean in the main stretch of Surfers Paradise called Billy's Beach House. A warm breeze was blowing gently over the water putting white caps on the waves lapping onto the sand that kept the ocean from rushing onto the street.

The ocean has always appealed to me. I find its relentless approach and retreat soothing and comforting and I love the pounding at the shoreline while sea birds walk on the packed sand. The mountains are another matter and I have no interest in winter sports especially those that require expensive equipment. I avoid activities that include speed, cold and heights where there is the possibility of falling down and breaking body parts. As fun as it sounds, it's never appealed to me. I'm never as happy as when I am close to ocean water. Not that I go *in* the water where there are all manner of stinging, biting, tentacled things, but I like to *look* at it

Miraculously, I found a park three spots down from the front door and a welcome burst of air-conditioning washed over me when I walked into the bar. A two-piece band by the name of 'Geek' was playing on a small platform and a group of teenagers were playing pool and swaying in time with the music while they sang along with the band. The music was good and several girls were surreptitiously eyeing off the dark-haired singer/drummer and the blonde guitarist doing back-up vocals. A group of women at a nearby table were talking loudly over each other and swilling red wine like they'd heard the grape harvest this year had failed.

Joseph Banner was sitting at the bar on a stool nursing what I knew to be a Jack Daniels on ice in one hand and a cigarette in the other hand. By the look of him, he'd been here for longer than he should have been. As I sat down on a stool next to him, he gave me a look, something you'd expect from Al Pacino.

I ordered a Jack Daniels of my own plus a burger and fries and said to him, "You look beat," as my drink arrived.

Joe was a solicitor who worked for a large firm in Surfers Paradise who had hired him three years ago with assurances that he would move into criminal law in a year or so. Instead, they buried him in corporate law. His job was to pull respectable businessmen out of the cracks they fall into when dealing with other respectable businessmen.

"I am," he said staring down at his drink. "I told the management committee on Friday I need help but they just said to make my people work harder." He shook his head. "Look at me. It's only Wednesday and I'm shattered."

"Why don't you leave? You could get a job anywhere you want."

"Nah. I'm getting too old to start over again. And don't forget, my wife is the boss's daughter and she loves wearing diamonds and silk while redecorating the house."

I caught a note of bitterness in Joe's tone, even though he gave me a crooked smile that showed teeth that were showing the first signs of nicotine discolouration. This side of Joe was something I wasn't used to hearing and I put it down to a fight with Sarah.

Sarah was Joe's second wife and twenty-five years younger than Joe but since they'd married six months ago, Joe has aged ten years and now looks sixty instead of fifty. Stupid is a word that comes to mind, but I would never say that to his face.

As if reading my thoughts, Joe said, "You think I'm crazy, don't you?"

My burger arrived and I started on it ravenously. I shook my head and wiped the sauce from my mouth with a serviette lying by the plate. "I didn't say that."

"Your silence is deafening,' he said, 'but what's done is done now."

The band started playing a Pearl Jam song and a loud cheer from kids at the pool table filled the room.

Joe squinted at me through cigarette smoke and waited for the noise to settle a little before continuing.

"My mother once said that you have to sleep in the bed that you make. It's character building."

He took a sip of his drink without taking the cigarette out of his mouth.

"It has its advantages, you know," he continued. "Sarah is hot and when she's happy, life is pretty good for me, too."

He looked at me over the top of his glasses while I ate. He was wearing a suit that must have cost him over three thousand dollars but there was cigarette ash down the front of his shirt and tie along with strands of hair that was fast disappearing off the top of his head. I'd never met an easier guy to be around. He never tried to hide his wealthy background, but his aura of casualness made everyone feel at ease. I like him for that.

He shrugged. "I had an itch and I scratched it."

"Same as Sally, I guess." I took another sip of my own drink. The burger had settled heavily in my stomach and I had a feeling I was going to regret eating it so fast. "You came out alright after your divorce though, Joe. You landed on your feet. You were lucky. Some of us are not so lucky. Sally could have taken all the money I had when she left. Instead, she took my daughter. Because of that, I haven't wished Sally too much good luck for a while now."

Someone shouted for a beer and the bartender, a dark-haired, dark-eyed Italian type with rings in his ear, nose and lip, began pouring from the tap.

"That's just revenge talking, my friend."

As he sat on the stool next to me, his brown eyes looked like they belonged to a dog behind a wire fence in the pound. Bassett hound bags under each eye.

He glanced up from his drink. "You seeing anyone yet?"

I had no wish to go along with this line of conversation. I shook my head and said, "Too busy, Joe."

He looked at me as if something had just occurred to him. "I know someone you might take a shine to. I've seen her a couple of times at work seminars. Dynamite woman. Short black hair, blue eyes, brilliant red lipstick, legs that went all the way up to here. Has a smile that glowed like a nuclear reactor." He put his finger in the air to tell the waiter he wanted another drink. The way he was slinging them back, he'd have to be carried out.

There was some loud applause coming from the patrons at the tables as the band finished a song. They nodded their thanks and started another song made famous by Kurt Cobain when he was alive and singing with Nirvana.

Joe glanced over his shoulder at them before continuing. "Okay, as I was saying. I was sipping my first glass of champagne after this medical seminar I attended and I was by an open door having a smoke when I saw her. She was a vision. The black dress she wore must have cost her a fortune." He was grinning as if the memory was a very pleasant one he didn't want to forget in a hurry. "Everything was absolutely perfect about her from the top of her shining hair to the six-inch heels she wore. You'd have loved her."

"You sound like you were taken with her yourself."

He gave a little chuckle as the waiter deposited another Jack Daniels in front of Joe and he nodded his thanks. Joe spun the glass around making little watermarks on top of the bar.

He lifted the glass to his lips and took a gulp. "On second thoughts. Maybe she's not for you. She had men turning to jelly at one look from her and she damn well knew it. Made you feel like you were the only one in the room that mattered. Worked the room beautifully."

"You make her sound scheming," I said.

"Aren't they all? Women, I mean. Know what they want and go for it. The next time I saw her was at a fundraiser for some charity or other. Set the scene in your mind. The room was full of businessmen. Everybody who was anybody was invited, and despite my reluctance to go, it was Sarah's idea mind you, the night turned out surprisingly enjoyable. The food was great, the champagne was bottomless and the music was unobtrusive." He took another gulp of his drink before continuing.

"In hindsight, something just wasn't quite right. I had the feeling that she was 'on' whenever a man looked at her, the way an actor would feel when the curtain raises on a stage production: everything deliberate and staged. She even spoke in a different tone when men were around. Believe me, she was no Susie Creampuff and she was no different from most women. But she was so sweet on the eye."

"Are you disillusioned with Sarah?" I asked.

He gave me a strange look before continuing. "Nah. She's tidying me up and I'm an old dog learning new tricks."

"Just don't slip up and pee on my leg."

"Jack," he said in a mock reprimand. "You're my friend."

A cigarette dangled from one corner of his lips as he talked, dropping ash onto the top of the bar. He swept the ash away with the back of his hand leaving a streak.

"I come here every afternoon before going home. Sarah won't let me smoke in the house. Says it leaves a smell over everything, including her." He took a deep drag on the cigarette then tilted his head back and blew the smoke into the air. "Also says it'll kill me one day." He gave a quick bark that doubled as a laugh. "Be glad for the rest."

The band finished the song and another roar of applause came from the pool table as Joe drained the rest of his glass and stood up. "Well, that's me. I'm off home to the little lady." He winked at me and grinned. "Make her happy and she'll make me happy."

"Your mother tell you that too?" I asked.

"It's good advice, Jack. Put it in your memory bank for later."

With a slap on the back, he was gone.

I drained my own glass and checked my watch. 10 o'clock. Time to head home. I had a big day tomorrow. First thing in the morning, I wanted to go over the files I'd retrieved by the Archives Department. I was going to need as much sleep as I could get.

15

The shrillness of the telephone jerked me awake. My sleep had been so deep, there was no slow swim to the surface. One moment I was drowning in black and the next, my heart was pounding and I was sitting bolt upright. I could feel a sheen of sweat running down the side of my face that wasn't there because of the summer humidity.

I groaned and rolled over as I picked up the receiver expecting it to be a call from the station informing me of another murder that had been committed somewhere on the streets of Surfers Paradise in the early hours of the morning. I could see it now. Men standing in bars, thigh to thigh, until tempers bubbled to the surface like the bubbles in their beer. Sunburn itching, already peeling. Girls leaving even though they'd been buying them drinks all night. A single moment of rage and ....

"Jack. Come on. It's me." Sam's voice sounded urgent with no sign of sleep in her voice. I glanced at the clock. 5.00 am.

"What?" I asked groggily into the mouthpiece as I blinked in the dark, fighting the impulse to fade back into sleep. "Sam?" I asked through the haze of sleep. I could almost see her shaking her hair and tucking it behind her ears absentmindedly as she spoke before wiping at the fine line between her eyebrows.

"Come on, Jack," she said. "Wake up."

That's when I noticed her voice trembling. This was new and so unlike Sam. She was the strongest woman I knew, totally confident in herself and her ability to do her work well, so this wavering voice was new to me.

"Sam? What's wrong?" I sat up swung my legs over the side of the bed before turning on the bedside lamp. "Okay. I'm awake. Talk to me."

I could hear her begin to sniffle and a thin sound like that of an injured kitten came from the earpiece.

"They found Joey's body, Jack. He's dead."

16

It was 6.30 am by the time I wound my way once more up Tamborine Mountain to find uniformed officers clearing the area. After Sam's call, I sat with the phone to my ear, listening until the dial tone returned. I sat there longer still, hearing the tone, waiting for it to tell me that the dead boy on Tamborine Mountain wasn't Joey Caruthers, waiting for it to tell me something else. Anything. Eventually, I dragged myself out of bed. Half an hour later, Sam picked me up and we made our way up the mountain for the fourth time in three days.

We passed several joggers on my way and pretty soon two patrol cars appeared, parked by the side of the road. Mary was heaving a metal box out of the back of a white van marked Surfers Paradise Medical Examiner stencilled on the side as we pulled up and she glanced up at us, looking tense. By the time we got out of the car, she had disappeared down a trail through the trees.

A patrolman standing close by with his arms folded recognised me and said, "Welcome back, sir." He jerked his head in Mary's direction. "Coroner just went down," he said, pre-empting any questions I had.

"I know," I replied. "We just saw her. Who found the body?"

"A couple of bushwalkers. Said they do this regularly but never in this area. The ground is too uneven and if one of them were to fall and twist an ankle, the other would have miles to walk for help."

"Where are the other policemen?" I asked, looking around and seeing no one.

"Checking out the terrain on the other side of the ridge."

"Who identified the body as Joey Caruthers?" I asked.

"The stupid hikers did."

He spoke the works with contempt and I had to agree with him. With all the crime shows on the television these days such as Law and Order and CSI, you'd think people would know not to touch the victim before the medical examiner has had a shot at it. That way when a suspect was brought to trial, the defence attorney couldn't argue that the evidence had been contaminated. As of now, that door was open.

"They found the kid with a backpack beside him and opened it up before calling it in first. Idiots." He almost spat the word. "The name was written in black niko pen on the inside flap. *Then* they called it in on a mobile." He shook his head angrily. "The guy on despatch remembered seeing the father in the station yesterday and he knew you and Detective Neil," he glanced in Sam's direction, "had interviewed him. He told them to wait until a unit got here and then called one of you. My partner and I were the closest in the area. When we got here, we confirmed that the boy was dead and asked for backup over the radio."

I saw a shadow cross his face as he glanced in the direction Mary had gone. I knew the image of Joey's small body would be burned in his memory for a long time to come.

"Okay." I said, bringing him back to the present. "I want you to go get the other patrolmen. I've got a job for them."

"Let me guess," he said, rolling his eyes. "Door to door."

I smiled a bitter smile. "You're clairvoyant. Let me know if anyone saw anything."

"Don't hold your breath. It's pretty isolated up here."

Sam and I both nodded before we followed the trail that Mary had taken along a ledge twenty-feet above a dry creek bed. Sam had been quiet on the trip up and as I glanced over at her, I could see her eyes had a red tinge to them from holding back tears.

In the distance, a church bell tolled. The sound was hollow, ringing casually in an area some god had clearly forgotten.

When we reached the yellow crime tape, we followed a freshly broken path down a narrow, winding trail through the trees. The leafy canopy above us rustled from the light breeze but down on the floor, the air was still. Specks of ash from the nearby fires to the west filtered through the canopy, floating in the still air.

In a small clearing, Mary was crouched over a small body.

Joey lay on his chest. His head was turned to the side and he seemed to be looking at something just over his shoulder. Even though thick bushes partially obscured his body, I could see his right arm was twisted behind him, his left arm extended straight out in front of him while his left leg was twisted at the knee. Mary began to tape both hands into a plastic bag to preserve any evidence that might be under the fingernails. From what I could see, the cheek resting on the ground was discoloured with lividity while the side turned upwards looked pale and drained of blood. The ugly smell of body gases were beginning to hang in the air while giant flies buzzed and swarmed around his already swelling body. Mary swatted at the flies with hands ensconced in yellow latex gloves as she occasionally wrote something down on a clipboard.

There was a loud shushing noise in my head and my voice didn't want to work. I cleared my throat and muttered, "Hello, Mary." Her eyes flicked up and then dropped back to the body. "How about an estimate on time of death?"

She tried to bend the boy's elbow joint. It was stiff but yielding. She looked up at me and said, "Rigor has started to let go so I'd say nearly twenty hours. I'll be able to tell more accurately in a few minutes."

She stood up and walked over to her metal box and removed a scalpel and a long metal thermometer before walking back to the body. I knew she was going to do a liver temperature and would chart it with the outside air temperature. From this, she would be able to tell how long the body had been cooling. Sam and I both turned away so we wouldn't have to see the procedure.

"I know this seems to fit in with the other boys but something's not right," I said more to myself than to Sam. "Joey's age is right. And there can't be a coincidence in the locality of his body." Cops just don't believe in coincidence. I heard *that* on 'Law and Order'. "So, why was Joey dumped here and not buried up with the others?" I asked.

I did a little mental arithmetic and suddenly I knew.

I turned to Sam. "The father said Joey went missing yesterday, right?"

I could see the muscles rigid beneath Sam's shirt and she clenched and unclenched her jaws as she nodded silently, trying to keep her emotions in check.

I looked up in the direction of where the other gravesites were, higher up on the mountain. "That means Joey was dumped here because *we* were up the mountain at the first crime scene unearthing the other boys. The killer couldn't bury Joey with the rest because *we* were already up there. Whoever did this panicked and left him here instead."

I looked around as I shook my head. "I almost hate to say this, but there's an element of craziness here. I mean, he turns up at the site that's surrounded by cops in broad daylight. So he has to find another site to dump the boy. But why would he pick one so close to the original site where the place is crawling with police and reporters? Wouldn't you think he'd get as far away from here as possible? He took all kinds of risks and any number of things could have gone wrong. Don't you think that shows an unstable mind?"

There was silence in response. When Sam didn't answer me straight away, I turned and looked into her eyes. They shone with unshed tears and her face was pale and pinched. I could see her throat swallowing over and over as if something was lodged there.

"You want to go back to the car?" I asked.

She nodded without saying anything and spun on her heels and stumbled away towards the car.

I turned to Mary. "What was the cause of death? Any signs of trauma?"

"No visible signs so far but Walt will be able to tell more after the autopsy."

I stood and watched as the photographer took photos around Joey in minute detail. As I stood, I swatted at the blowflies all too aware of where they had been. I really didn't want to be standing there and finally, Mary stood up and released the body to her crew. They zipped Joey into a blue plastic body bag, strapped the body to a stretcher, then she, her crew and the photographer worked their way up the slope with me in tow.

Sam was sitting sideways in the front passenger side seat, her feet on the ground beside the car. She looked up at me as I crunched my way over to the car then swung her feet inside before slamming the door.

"Are you alright?" I asked as I turned the car around onto the road, heading back to the station.

"Peachy," she said as she stared out the window.

We drove for a while in silence until I felt I had to say something.

"You have to divorce yourself from emotion, Sam."

Sam continued looking out of the passenger side window, her eyes settling on no one spot for more than a second. Outside, the sun shone like a perfect ball of fire in a perfect blue sky.

I turned by gaze from the road for a second and looked at her. "Are you listening to me?" I asked.

I could see her shoulders rising and falling sporadically, and I knew she was struggling to keep herself together.

"I said, are you listening to me? We have to remain focused! If we don't, he wins."

Her head snapped to face me. "Shut up, Jack. Leave me alone for a while." The voice that emerged was that of a hurt 6-year-old and I felt my heart tug. But this was no time for the luxury of sympathy at her distress and she wouldn't thank me later for giving in to her.

"Point your gun at someone else, Sam. I'm not the one you should be angry at, okay?"

"I have to take it out on someone. I can't take it out on the lunatic who did this!"

"Don't call him a lunatic." My voice came out in a whisper as I kept my eyes fixed on the winding road. "Don't make that mistake. This guy is usually methodical, exacting and most of all patient. Something happened to change that."

"So what does that little voice in your head say?"

"Usually, it says what are you asking *me* for?"

She breathed deeply. "But what about now?"

"It's telling me *we* ruined his plan. Ten years ago, he killed a boy and buried him here. For some reason, every 2nd January starting five years ago, he has abducted another boy and killed him, burying him with the others. It's a ritual that we don't understand, sure, but it's a ritual that means something to him. Now that we've broken that ritual, I don't know what he's going to do. The fat lady is all dressed up and ready to sing. I just don't know what the words are yet."

Sam sat quietly beside me, her clothing and hair perfect. Her expression, however, had become vacant. Her feelings, whatever they were, were not on display anymore. This affected me more than tears and hysterics.

"Sam, concentrate. Focus on the facts and ask yourself what made him change his m.o. Try to thing of anything, no matter how insignificant it may seem. Even things that may seem irrelevant may lead us to something important."

Most murders aren't solved by clues like you see on Hill Street Blues, or forensics like you read in Patricia Cornwall books. The truth is that almost all murders are solved when somebody drops a clue. Like when someone says, 'Billy said he was going to kill him' and we go to Billy's place and find the murder weapon hidden under Billy's mattress. Cut and dried. But when there isn't anyone to point the finger at Billy, Billy gets away. So far, there hadn't been any finger-pointing, but that has never stopped me before.

I glanced quickly towards her and saw her eyes set on mine. She sighed the way you sigh when you've been holding your breath at a horror movie.

We travelled a while longer in silence, lost in our own thoughts. I leant forward and switched on the radio. Classical music that sounded like it was made up entirely of mistakes came out of the speakers.

"German," I said as we drove. "I can't stand German opera. You?" I asked.

"I don't know much about opera," she said to the windscreen.

"Ponderous. Wagner may have been a genius but his operas are ponderous. French is too fluffy. Russian is repetitive. I don't listen to opera too much but from what I've heard, it was made for Italians."

"Like I said, I don't know much about opera."

I turned the radio off and looked out my window. I'd checked the weather report before leaving home this morning. The rain was supposed to hit Surfers today and as I looked at the clear sky and burning sun, my faith in the Channel 9 weather girl was once again shaken.

Up ahead, I saw a small coffee shop so I pulled over.

"Let's have a break."

I parked the car and we both waled in silence past a picnic table, its surface covered in small splinters sticking out of the wood like bristles from a brush. The day was growing more humid around us and I knew by midday it would feel like I was breathing water. We kept walking.

The place depended on natural lighting so it was a dark on the inside. The only one other person in the coffee shop sat about twenty feet away with his back against the wall, one hand on the table, legs crossed at the ankles, reading a paper and sipping his coffee without looking at the cup. He was wearing khaki pants and a light-weight white shirt and he glanced up at us as we walked in then looked back down at his paper again.

We sat opposite each other and I rested my forearms on the table in the universal pose of travellers everywhere. The coffee smelled fresh and I could hear eggs and bacon sizzling in the kitchen.

A waitress came over to our table.

"Can I help you?" she asked as she pushed chewing gum to one side of her mouth.

"Yeah," I said. "A double decaf skinny moccachino made on soy milk with nutmeg on top."

"What about a little maraschino cherry?" she asked. Just like that. No hesitation. No smile.

"No thanks. I'm on a diet."

She sighed heavily and thrust one hip impatiently to the side and continued chewing, waiting.

"Two flat whites," I said, suitably abashed.

When she left to fill the order, I turned back to Sam. "You can't solve the world's problems, Sam. Don't even try."

She gave me a disgusted look. "I understand that. And before you go on, I know we all have a time set for us to die. Right now, it's *when* you die that's bothering me." She hesitated, "when those little *boys* died, more to the point. It wasn't their turn yet. Someone made it that way."

I nodded. "I know. If you're in an accident, you get yourself patched up. You're in charge of your own life and safety. But these kids didn't have that luxury because some battles just can't be won."

Sam was staring at me with a frown furrowed on her brow.

"Don't think I haven't thought about this very carefully. I remember when my father died. He had terminal cancer and didn't tell me about it until it was too late. I asked him why and he said, *'Because it's my time to go.'* I remember arguing with him that he could have had treatment and that he was being too passive but he wouldn't listen to me. I even asked him *'But won't you miss me?'*"

My hands were flat on the table as I remembered that conversation with my father. The waitress came with our coffees and put them down in front of us without saying a word. Sam's eyes roamed the contours of my face barely noticing the coffee.

I stared off into the trees as I picked my cup up and took a sip before continuing. "*'Wrong question'*, he said to me. *'I'll be dead. I won't be missing anyone or anything. It's you who'll miss me. Like you miss your brother. Like I miss him. Like you'll miss your mother one day. It's a part of life, missing the dead.'*"

I remember those words as if it were today. *'Like you miss your brother'*. When my younger brother was small, I assumed the part of the vigilant, protective brother, certain that throughout our lives I would be there to protect him. I'd already caught him as he tumbled from chairs and staircases, tugged him away from blazing hearths, snatched his fingers from closing doors. His smile was a light aimed at the world. My father used to scold me. *'He can't avoid getting hurt, Jack,'* he said. *'Next time, let him fall.'* When he didn't come back from Afghanistan, I think he remembered those words with deep regret and would have given his own life if I'd been able to save him just one more time.

I looked up at Sam and continued. "Then he said to me, *'What you're asking me is how can I abandon you? Have I lost interest in you?'* And he was right. I had been thinking those exact words. He said dying and leaving loved ones behind is like walking out of a movie that's not finished yet and you're really enjoying. You'll never know the ending. He said he'll never know what happens to me and that was the worst part for him. But then he realised that he was going to walk out of the movie sooner or later anyway and it will still be going long after he's gone. Then it didn't seem to matter that much to him."

We sat in silence for a while, sipping our coffees.

"They were all so young, you know?" she said sadly. "I keep thinking of my own kid and how I'd feel if someone took him."

"They were young, yes. But if they'd been twenty or forty, it wouldn't be any better. Death is death and murder is murder. Don't make it any worse by getting sentimental about their ages, Sam."

She waved a spoon in my direction. "I know what you're saying, Jack. But the fact remains that those little boys should still be alive."

"Yes, they should." My coffee had cooled but I took a sip anyway before putting the cup down on the saucer. "But there's nothing we can do about that now. They're gone. But this is where we *do* come in. We stay focused on our job and we find that son-of-a-bitch before he does this again to another boy."

She had been staring at the coffee dregs in the bottom of her cup as I watched a small frown deepen her forehead. She glanced up and caught me watching her.

She gave me a watery smile. "Don't worry about me. I'll be fine."

I gave her a surprised look, like I didn't know what she was talking about. "I'm just checking you out, Neil. Purely sexist, nothing more."

She leaned back in her chair and gave me a better smile.

"So, what now?" she asked softly.

"To quote an old proverb, before we go forward, we have to go back."

17

I turned the car around the last corner leading to the station as a warm breeze blew gently over the water, putting white caps on the waves lapping onto the sand that kept the ocean from rushing onto the street.

I could see a dozen people that could only be reporters converged around the entrance of the station. A van from a television network with a microwave dish perched on top spat out a few more reporters as we drew closer. A cameraman for a Brisbane television station saw us and swung his camera around, knocking a blonde female talent off kilter. She stumbled and shot him a nasty look before running towards us with her microphone held out in front as we pulled up to the kerb. In seconds, everyone was talking at once.

"Shit," Sam mumbled as she opened the door pushing several reporters away at the same time. Everyone was running and yelling and I had an almost overwhelming urge to put the car in gear and drive off.

A seagull hovered in the breeze and as he floated past, he looked down at me. I made my right hand into a gun and pointed it at him. He banked away quickly from the building and disappeared. If only reporters were that easy to get rid of.

"Can you tell us about the body found on Mount Tamborine, Sergeant?"

"No," I said as I pushed forward.

"Can you give us a statement, sir?"

"No."

"Come on Sergeant," I heard another say, "give us a break."

"No."

"Do we have a serial killer loose on the Gold Coast, Sergeant Curtis?" the blonde asked.

"Do you have any suspects yet, sir?" yelled an Asian man.

Sam pushed her way towards the entrance and left me to deal with them. I held my hands up in the air trying to be heard.

"Quiet down! Quiet! Calm down!" I said. People were still yelling. "CALM DOWN!" I yelled at them back at them.

I looked around and a modicum of hush settled.

"Now here's how it's going to go. I'll answer questions for five minutes and five minutes only. If those questions don't come in a sane, calm and orderly fashion, I'm out of here. I will NOT discuss the details of this investigation, so don't bother asking."

The climbing sun was fast becoming a torch in the sky and heat soaked my shoulders and face until I could feel a delicate trickle of sweat running through my hair. I glanced at my watch. "Okay. Go."

Five minutes later and true to my word, I was pushing my way into the air-conditioning. They hadn't appreciated my vague answers to their questions, but that's the way it goes sometimes.

I walked down the same short hall I do every day, up the familiar flight of stairs and into the same squad room. People still came in and went out. An overweight policewoman bought a coke that wasn't a diet coke and another cop led a young teenager through the swinging doors to the holding cells. Empty doughnut boxes littered desks surrounded by empty styrofoam coffee cups, half of which had cigarette butts soaking up the coffee dregs on the bottom. After what I'd seen this morning, I had expected things to be different somehow.

I asked Pete where Sam was and he told me she was sitting with Frank Caruthers in Interrogation Room 1. As I walked past, I saw Sam staring out the window somewhere around the orbit of Jupiter. Frank Caruthers looked up at me hopefully, as if I were going to tell him it was all a terrible mistake. That it wasn't Joey up on the mountain. That it was someone else's little boy. Some other child who'd been abducted and murdered then left for dead in the scrub.

For years, being a cop has taught me that families hold fiercely to whatever little hope they can find. For instance, if their daughter was on a plane that crashed, they would wonder if perhaps she'd missed her flight or given her seat away to someone else and she'd be back with them soon.

One look at my face and he dropped his chin back onto his chest and let the tears fall harder. With just one look, I had ended the last remnants of hope that had ridden in the back of his mind like a stone in his shoe. I had unburied Joey's remains and left his father's hope tidily in their place.

The hard thing about death is that nothing ever changes. The hard thing about life is that nothing ever stays the same.

18

While Sam sat with Joey's father, I went back to my desk and sat down. The five files I'd separated from the others were still on my desk where I'd left them the night before. I put the remaining ones I didn't need anymore in my 'out' tray with a note tagged to them to be returned to the Archives Department.

What I needed was to identify the five boys found on the mountain, which meant going to see the five sets of parents who'd made the missing persons reports in the files I had on my desk. I wouldn't have time to get around to all them today but I could make a good start while I waited for Joey's autopsy report to come in. I picked up two of the files, left a note for Sam to say where I was going and for her to start contacting the parents of the others to organise a time for us to interview them.

Halfway out the door, I remembered that my first job should be to speak to Angela Ashton. As difficult as it was going to be without any forensic findings, I needed to confirm the fact that the body was indeed that of Peter Ashton.

The absence of any report in itself was highly suspicious. There were also a lot of questions I wanted to ask beginning with *why* a missing persons report hadn't been made ten years ago, how he sustained all the injuries Doctor Mason had found on the tiny skeleton and how could a parent inflict so much pain on to a small child. I also needed to find a connection to someone who knew about the other murders and the best place to start was at the beginning.

I'm going to get you, I thought again.

Sam had already checked and found that the address was still current for Angela's father, so I backtracked to my desk, found the file with the birth report and wrote the address of Douglas Ashton down in my notebook.

I added a p.s. to the note I left Sam and started off again.

Since it was 11 o'clock and all I'd had all day was a cup of coffee with Sam, I bought a packet of pre-made sandwiches at a nearby take-away and ate them as I drove to the Isle of Capri.

19

The road from Surfers Paradise to the Isle of Capri is dotted with motels, fast food outlets, restaurants and more motels. It was bright and sunny and the morning heat shimmered off the roads and cars giving it an illusion of a silver lining. White gulls floated and circled overhead and girls in minuscule bikinis soaked up the sun with no regard for the ads on television about slip, slop and slapping. Surfers Paradise is Australia's answer to 77 Sunset Strip. Paradise.

My route took me past tower blocks, then town houses and gradually past run-down units that had been turned into holiday residences. It was like two worlds with one simple division: those with money and those with very little. The strange part was that they lived side by side.

It wasn't just material worth either: a big house, a new car, a boat, a profession. Money bought more than that. It bought control. The judges and the judged. The rulers and the ruled. Those who made fashion and those who followed it. The two understood each other even if they didn't like each other and they understood the inequalities.

But in my job, I've learnt that there is a third group. Those who would not agree and would not be ruled. Those who would kill you for your money or your car or even for your mobile phone. They would even kill you if you got in their way or just because they felt like it. Like every city,

Surfers Paradise has all these types of people and I work both sides of the street.

I pulled up at a set of lights behind an eight-wheeler truck with a bumper sticker that read, *'God is my co-pilot'*. On the green light, he and God pulled away doing about 80 in a 60 zone.

Once I turned onto The Promenade at the Isle of Capri, I pulled my car up to a newly erected security gate house protecting the estate. A guard stepped out, eyed the car up and down, then me, and gave me a forced smile.

"You lost or something?" he asked.

I tried to give him a pleasant smile in return but I had a feeling it would only made me look like something had turned sour in my mouth.

"I'd like to talk to a Douglas Ashton. I believe he still lives here?"

"Does Mr Ashton know you're coming?"

"Not unless he's psychic," I quipped.

He eyed me for a second, one eyebrow cocked, while he digested the glib answer. "Hold on a minute."

He returned to the gatehouse and I saw him pick up a phone. While he talked, I looked through the windscreen at some of the homes visible from my position. They were all huge with manicured lawns big enough to play touch football on. A had a good idea that the sun would be glistening off swimming pools in every single back yard while boats of every shape and size bobbed at pontoons.

The guard came out and put a hand on the roof of the car.

"He wants to know what it's about."

"Tell him I'll discuss it with him at the house. In private. Tell him I have a court order." I didn't have one, but he didn't have to know that.

The guard shrugged his shoulders in a have-it-your-own-way gesture and went back inside the gatehouse. I watched him speaking for a few more moments. When he hung up, the gate slowly started to open and he waved me in.

"Straight on," he said, mimicking a gravelly-voiced Siri from my iPhone.

Towards the end of the street, I could see a house with the architectural equivalent of a circus tent: white concrete with a roof broken into triangular wedges supported by a circular pole and three gaily-painted pipes. My guess was that the inside floors would be aggregate. Add some corrugated iron panels and you'd have the kind of house Metropolitan Homes might refer to as 'unsparing', 'inspired' or 'brilliantly iconoclastic'. 'Unremittingly tacky' would also cover it, in my opinion.

I checked the address and saw my destination was four houses down.

The Ashton house was made to look like a big Italian villa set behind a wrought-iron fence and hidden by enormous tropical palms, bird-of-paradise plants as big as giraffes and lush green tree ferns wilting in the heat. A statue of the Venus De Milo stood in the middle of a circular water feature big enough to sail a decent sized yacht around while koi the size of marlin swam lazily in the depths.

A maid greeted me at the door and looked me up and down before taking my business card. She shut the door on my face and left me standing on the front porch while the sun beat down on my back. I could feel sweat running down my back and wetness under my armpits and I resisted the urge to sniff them in case someone was looking.

She returned and allowed me to enter, leading me down a long hallway towards a set of double doors standing open at the far end. My shoes clacked with military crispness on the polished wooden floor, sounding almost like hooves, and as I walked, I did what I do best. I snooped.

The roof of the entrance was the size of a small cathedral, with a 20-foot ceiling and Persian carpets as far as the eye could see. Ugly paintings, probably worth a small fortune, watched me from above as I clip-clopped my way down the hallway. Richly coloured furnishings all sang of 'old wealth' and the unequivocally rich. There were no photographs of family vacations, no school portraits and no shots of the Mr and Missus with the kids decked out for the camera. There wasn't even one pizza box in sight.

"Thank you, Mrs Benson," rasped a voice through an open doorway I suspected lead to a study.

Douglas Ashton was sitting behind a massive oak desk in a wheel chair dressed in a blue smoking jacket. He did not come around to meet me and I didn't make a move towards him.

Mrs Benson stood by the door, hands at her side, with no expression on her face.

I'd met other Douglas Ashtons before. He would be the sort of person to complain about welfare mothers and government handouts and how they should get up and do something about their plight instead of whingeing about it while he himself earned his own money the old-fashioned way. He inherited it. He belonged to the class of entitled super wealthy who delude themselves into believing they earned their money with hard work. We all live with self-justification but if you've never fended for yourself and your family, if you live in luxury and have done nothing to deserve it, then don't be such a prig about it.

I stood. He sat. Mrs Benson remained standing.

He waved me impatiently to a chair on the other side of the desk and I did as I was told. As I sat and stared at him, he stared straight back at me. Cats, both wild and domestic, watch with unblinking regard, alert for the smallest variation in posture, the minutest shift of attention. He had that intensity.

He had a plump, well-fed look that was soft around the edges and a ruddy complexion. His brooding black eyes were set into a long bony face and instead of a cigarette, a cigar was resting unlit in an ashtray by his elbow. He laced his fingers over his paunch and looked at me as if I was badly erected window dressing. He was someone who understood the power of being totally focussed on the person in his presence. No subtle glances at his watch, no surreptitious shift in gaze taking in my attire. He would be as patient as a cat watching a crack in a rock where a lizard had disappeared.

Seconds passed before he glanced up at Mrs Benson.

"You may return to your duties, thank you Mrs Benson."

His attention was back to me. He puffed out his cheeks, sat back in his chair and regarded me for a few seconds, before saying, "I can't tell you how embarrassed I am to have that car of yours in my driveway."

My eyebrows raised and I blinked a few times, I know I did that, because I was a little taken aback. "Well, Mr Ashton," I said slowly, "I'm pretty embarrassed myself but the Ferrari is in getting the tow bar re-chromed, so what do you do?"

He held my eyes for a moment. "The guard said you had a court order. May I see it?"

"The guard must have misunderstood me." I'd like to think that I remained cool and calm as I spoke. "I told him we could *get* a court order, if you refused to see me."

He harrumphed sarcastically. "I'm sure you did," he replied, the tone of his voice letting me know he didn't believe me for a second. "How may I help you, Sergeant?"

"You have a daughter by the name of Angela, Mr Ashton?"

"Yes." His reply was drawn out and had a wariness to it.

"Our records show, sir, that she gave birth to a child twenty years ago."

He stared at me in amazement. "Is that why you're here? Because my ungrateful daughter made a mistake and got herself pregnant twenty years ago?" He was shaking his head from side to side. "Things must be awfully slow at that police station of yours."

His voice held anger and I could see the man he'd been before he was in the chair. A no-nonsense man who could intimidate the best of them and make anything sound plausible.

"I have read somewhere," he began again, "that no one is born evil and that no one is inherently bad. My answer to that is simply to look into the heart of Angela. It is black. Or at least it was the last time I saw her twelve years ago. She has not bothered to contact me and the feeling I have for her is mutual."

He wheeled his chair from around the side of the desk and spun it towards me. "My daughter had a child, yes, but I had it legally adopted before she could see it. As far as I know, Sergeant, that is not against the law."

"You had the boy adopted?" I hadn't expected that. "At birth?"

He eyed me up and down with a look of derision on his face. "Yes. At birth. I have no idea what you could possibly want with that piece of information and I really don't care. That part of our lives is over so why don't you go back to that station of yours and earn that taxpayer's money we give you."

I tried not to let him see the anger building up inside but it was hard to do when I knew my face was red. I had known many men who acted strong like this but they always had a core of weakness. Something deep inside. Their harsh exterior was usually a shield against the pain that was buried inside their hearts. Most times, *they* weren't the guilty ones. It was the timid ones who proved capable of accomplishing terrible things.

I drew a few even steady breaths, listening to the birds in the trees outside. When I spoke, I kept my voice even and lowered.

"Mr Ashton. We have recently unearthed the remains of a child's body on Tamborine Mountain. The boy was buried about ten years ago and would have been about ten years old at the time. We now know that that child was the boy your daughter delivered at Southport Hospital."

I searched his face for a sign of emotion and for a second, I thought I detected something. Every crease and line deepened on his face and seemed magnified by something incomprehensibly sharp and painful. This man had made a decision for his daughter and now his grandchild had been murdered. There was so much pain visible on his face that it was hard to look at him. And then, just as suddenly, the look was gone.

He shifted in his seat but his eyes never left my face. "This is something that doesn't concern us anymore, Sergeant. Children's Services are the ones you should be in contact with. They will have all the details of the adoption. I'm not sure what it is I can do for you."

I nodded slowly. "Totally correct, Mr Ashton, Children's Services will certainly be receiving a visit from us."

Maybe it was my own expression, but I saw his face darken somehow. He stared at me and I stared back, like a couple of mind readers trying to read the other one's thoughts.

"I'd like to speak to your daughter, Mr Ashton. I know you have had no contact with her, but do you know where I could find her?"

His face was the colour of dried blood and he breathed heavily before speaking. "As I said, she and I have not spoken for twelve years. We had an argument and she moved out. I have not seen or heard from her since and I do not know where she is."

His face had begun to sag with a look of permanent weariness that I recognise from my own reflection. He was an old man who'd seen too much and run out of emotional energy to deal with the burdens they already carry, much less any new ones. I couldn't judge him on it because I'd come close to cracking myself over the years.

In his youth, I imagine he'd been decisive, humourless and testy with a passion for getting the job done right. Now, he was beginning to look tired with dark pouches heavy under each eye. As he spoke, he seemed even more tired.

His cigar had been resting unlit in the ashtray at his elbow as he talked and I waited as he took out a lighter and lit it up again. He exhaled a mouthful of blue smoke before spinning his wheelchair around to stare out of the window overlooking the expanse of garden and Ginung Island in the distance.

"She was always impulsive," he said with a tone of irritation. "Never happy with anything I did. If I told her the sky was blue, she'd argue that it was green. I never knew how to handle her."

He snorted. "Her mother left us when Angela was barely three years old. Just up and left without saying why and where she was going. Left me a note saying she had to find out who she really was." He glanced over at me. "What the hell is that supposed to mean?"

I just shook my head and let him talk. Sometimes that's the best way the uncover facts. If you're lucky, they let something slip they wouldn't normally tell you. Then you add two and two together.

He looked back out the window again. "I did the best I could with Angela but she was always a handful. She was always getting into trouble at school and then one day she came home and told me she was pregnant. Just like that. Defiant. Said she was going to keep the baby and give it the life that she hadn't had."

He swung his chair back to face me. "But she was only sixteen and a minor so *I* made the decision for her. I had the child adopted."

Silence hung heavily in the room. Somewhere a clock ticked loudly and I could hear a distant drone that could have been a vacuum cleaner.

"She never forgave me." He almost spat the words out. "Ungrateful as always." He squared his shoulders defiantly. "I have no idea of where she is nor do I wish to know. She has made her own life now and she must live with it."

I folded my notebook and put it in my pocket before standing up.

"A few words to the wise, Sergeant," he said with a wry smile. "Firstly: I don't care what you think. Secondly: I would like to see a result as well. And I hope it will be soon. I'm well aware of what goes on in a police station. Every six months, you pull out the file of an unsolved crime, blow off the dust and write 'No new developments'. Then you put it back in the pile and call it 'Due Diligence'. I do not want that to happen with this case. I don't want this gathering dust like that cheap suit you pulled out of the closet to come and see me. And I don't want excuses about other cases and workload."

I took the insult about the suit because I had to. I nodded like I agreed with him and he let me wait while I digested the information.

"Thirdly," he added, "don't base your case on the ravings of someone like Angela who has a retarded perception of life. Be careful with any information she gives you. She is not the most stable person to talk to. She was always neurotic and high-strung."

My bad angel was yelling 'Up yours' but I managed to keep my voice even as I said, "Thank you for the advice. I'll try to remember that."

As if I hadn't said anything, he continued. "She lies about everything, Sergeant. So whatever story she's been telling you, chances are it's a lie. My advice is, don't go making a fool of yourself, falling for it. You wouldn't be the first and I don't suppose you'll be the last."

"Thanks for the advice."

I tried to keep the sarcasm out of my voice but I knew I'd failed.

He harrumphed and reached over to push a buzzer somewhere near the phone and the vacuum cleaner stopped. "Now if you don't mind, I'd like to be left alone if you have no more questions."

Seconds later, Mrs Benson stood at the door. I stood up and mumbled something that could have been taken as either a thank you or just clearing my throat.

Mrs Benson led me back down the hallway without saying a word and opened the door for me to leave. A chill ran down my back and I was glad to be outside in the nuclear heat again. I took two steps then turned around to face her. She was maybe 60 years old and comfortable with her surroundings, which could mean she'd been working here for a long time.

"Did you know Angela, Mrs Benson?"

She hesitated and glanced over her shoulder before stepping out onto the portico and half closed the door. She took a deep breath before answering me.

"Yes, I did," she whispered with a nod. It was the first words I'd heard her speak and I was surprised to hear the melody in it, like she had been a singer in her youth and the lilting quality had never left her voice. Probably a little Irish in there as well.

"Have you any idea where I can find her?"

She nodded. "She runs a coffee shop in Surfers Paradise. It's called The Coffee Cove. I've been in there a few times and passed the time with her but she does not want her father to know where she is." She glanced at the door again and listened before continuing. "She was a good girl but her past..." She shook her head and left the rest of the sentence unfinished.

"She was unhappy?" I asked.

She nodded again. "And she cracked. Her whole life had been like a bad movie and she was one of those child actors."

I didn't say anything, hoping she'd continue.

"It's like they play a part for as long as they can, but they're fighting a battle against their hormones and they can't win. One day they wake up and they're no longer kids and they just drown."

She watched me through hooded eyes. "Your past," she asked me, "are you completely settled with everything that ever happened in it? Or are there things that you don't talk about and that make you wince years later?"

I considered the question. Everyone has those kind of memories. Mine included a broken marriage that I blamed myself for, and a child that I'd neglected for two years, before getting in touch with her again. I remembered Sally's face as she left me, that look of weary resignation, and it was like that look drove a nail into my brain. Even now, when I talk to Jazz, I feel a wave of shame so total, it threatens to crumble me in its clenched fist.

And that was just one memory. The list was long, accrued over a lifetime of mistakes and bad judgments and impulses.

"I can see it in your face," she nodded again. "You've got pieces of your life you haven't reconciled. The thing is we all do. We all carry our past and we all mess up our present and we all have days when we don't see much point in struggling on towards our future. Angela was no different in that respect than everyone else. With her, losing that baby was the final straw that broke her back. She was the saddest person I have come across in a long time. Almost dying from all that sadness. I used to tell her that her father really did love her but he just didn't know how to show it. She stayed here with him for a few years after the adoption but the circumstances of her past caught up to her and she couldn't stay any longer."

"The circumstances of her past?" I asked.

She gave a sad smile. "What I told Angela about her father loving her? It was just words to soothe a lonely, sad girl. There was no love in this house. That little girl grew up with a bitter man who had no love in his heart for anyone." She gave a little shrug. "So she left and started a life of her own. I'm not saying she's happy but at least *she* has control of it now."

I stood on the walkway for a few seconds longer and nodded.

"Her final words to me as she left were, 'No one loves.'"

I thanked Mrs Benson for her time and walked slowly to my car.

No one loves.

20

As I'd told Douglas Ashton, I wanted to talk to Children's Services requesting them to pull the file on Peter Ashton so that we could find the name and address of his adoptive parents. From experience, I knew that I could expect little co-operation from Children's Services without a court order to release the information. But court orders take time and that was a luxury I didn't have.

If we were wrong and Peter Ashton was alive and well and a young man of twenty, then we would know to begin looking elsewhere. But if we were right in our assumptions that both boys were one in the same child, then these people were murderers and had gotten away with it for ten years. Chances were that they had moved after the boy's death. But if they'd felt confident that the boy's body was well hidden, they might still be living on the Gold Coast or even in Brisbane. A lot of *ifs* and *buts* but that's that way it goes sometimes.

I parked in the basement of the Children's Services building situated on the main Gold Coast Highway at Mermaid Beach. A black board with white stick-on alphabet letters in the foyer told me that Children's Services was situated on the second floor. I pushed the lift button and a door opened immediately. As they closed, a techno-instrumental version of *Hey Jude,* that I bet John Lennon would not have approved of, played while the lift took me skywards.

The lift door opened onto a corridor and directly in front of me were glass doors with '**Children's Services**' stencilled in gold on them. I opened the doors and walked through into a corridor.

By the look of it, Children's Services was designed so that you saw nothing but a hallway running in both directions with a lot of doors coming of it. I read a sign in front of me that said, '**Reception**' with an arrow pointing to the left. I headed in that direction.

The receptionist looked up from her computer and smiled at me with the genuineness of a politician's wife and asked sweetly, "Yes sir? How can I help you?"

She asked me to have a seat when I told her I wanted to see the person in charge and no I didn't have an appointment and yes, I'd wait.

Ten minutes later, the receptionist told me that Deputy Assistant in Charge Bettina Lawler – that's exactly how she said it, the full title - would see me now. She opened the door and I walked into Bettina Lawler's office.

"Please take a seat," she said, motioning me to one of two leather chairs.

Bettina Lawler's dark hair was pulled back into a neat French braid that extended just past her shoulder blades. Her black pants were wrinkled from sitting and over them she wore a white tailored shirt with the hem covering the waistband. Everything screamed functional and no-nonsense.

Her office was as serviceable as her attire. One desk, two chairs, a faded Monet print of waterlilies hanging on the wall behind her and a view out the window of the parking lot. That was pretty much it.

"How may I help you?" she asked, settling herself in her chair.

I spent the next five minutes telling her about the bodies of boys, how we connected them and how we'd discovered the name of the first boy from the hospital records. Through the whole speech, she sat ramrod straight in her chair, hands folded on the table in front of her.

"What I need from your department is the name and address of the adopting parents of Peter Ashton," I concluded.

She leant back and shook her head slightly. "I'm sorry, Sergeant. I can't do that."

I gave her my baffled look. "I'm sorry? Why is that?"

"This is a matter of confidentiality." Her voice held a sharp reproof as if I should know better than to even ask.

My mother always said that you catch more flies with honey than you do with vinegar but so far, vinegar had always worked much better than honey for me. I decided to play the tough cop while my good and bad angel battled it out.

"Ms Lawler," I began slowly, "we believe this enquiry may lead to the murderer of six boys. Be assured that we'll be discrete in this investigation. We simply want to find out if Peter Ashton is still alive. If he went missing ten years ago and no report was made, *then* we'll begin to ask certain questions and confidentiality goes out the window." I looked at her for a second before adding, "As I'm sure you well know."

"As I said, this information is confidential." She waved at her filing cabinets and the computer sitting on her desk. "You can't just walk in here off the streets, even if you are a policeman, and request sensitive information like this."

My good angel was saying, *Told you so*.

"A man in your position should be well aware of that," she continued. "I have the privacy and the rights of the child to think of."

She spoke the words firmly her back once again straight in the chair, not exactly uptight but comfortable only when things were in their proper place. I wondered if she had ever had a gleam in her eye when she was young. Right now, she looked like Suzie Homemaker, her hair gleaming with silver strands and her lips pursed together in a disapproving way. Had she ever been spontaneous or outrageous, even inappropriate? Had she ever had a wild stage in her youth, sneaking around with the local bad boy? I couldn't even begin to imagine it as she looked at me over the top of her glasses the way Mrs Williamson, my 5th grade teacher, used to do. Even when I hadn't done anything wrong, Mrs Williamson had a way about her that made me think I had.

"Let's not make this any more difficult that it already is," I said in my own stern voice. "This child is dead so there's no question of his rights being violated anymore. They already have been. This guy has a taste for his work and his confidence is growing." I eyed her in silence for a moment. "If I have to," I continued, "I can make just one phone call and half an hour later, you'll have the fax of a court order from a judge in your hand. To save time, how about you just help me find out as much as I can about the boy and let me get on with my job."

She gave a long, irritated sigh and tried to stare me down. I stared right back at her. What she didn't know was how obstinate and persistent I could be and that if I believed something wasn't right, I fixed it any way I could. Life can't be handled with a giant question mark over your head.

"You are in no position to make demands, Sergeant," she said, her eyes steady.

I stood up and said, "I'm not about to let this man kill another child. That will be on your conscience. I walked away from the table. "It's been a pleasure, Ms Lawler."

If I made it to the door, I'd have to get the court order and come back, a waste of precious time that I didn't have.

"Sergeant Curtis," her resigned voice called.

I was three feet or so from the door and my faith in human nature was restored.

I turned to face her. "Are you going to tell me you won't help me with my investigation?"

She gave another deep sigh and began clicking the keys on her computer. Some of the best victories are the ones you have to fight hard for.

She clicked one last button, then waited while the computer thought about what she wanted it to do. Seconds later, I saw the blue reflection of the screen mirrored in her glasses. She read silently, then looked up at me.

"Do you want me to print this out for you?" As if she was asking if I wanted milk and sugar in my coffee.

"Thank you," I nodded meekly.

The printer made a couple of burps and buzzes and spat two sheets of paper out into a tray. She handed them to me with a look of disapproval on her face.

"I can't say I approve of your methods, Sergeant."

"We gots to do what we gots to do," I said in my best Popeye voice.

She stared back at me silently. Maybe she'd never heard of Popeye and Bluto.

"There are channels, Sergeant," she said. "That's what I told the child's birthmother when she came in to see me."

"Peter Ashton's birth mother came in to see you?" I stared at her open-mouthed. "When was this?"

She looked back at the computer screen and clicked a couple of times then looked back up at me. "Eleven years ago."

I blinked a few times. I know I did. "And you remember what you said to her?"

"It's my job, Sergeant. Just like you have yours, I have mine. And I consider it an important one. I made a notation of the visit in my files." She nodded at the screen of her computer. "The violation of these children's rights is an extremely serious crime and I take my job seriously. I also have a good memory for certain things."

The image of Mrs Williamson flashed in front of my eyes again and I mentally tried to shake the image out of my mind of the overweight teacher my classmates and I had called Big W.

"Did you give her the names and the address of the child's adoptive parents?"

"Rules have changed since 2014. If you have proof of identity, you can request the address of your adopted child in the hope that you may have contact with them either through this department or through a group such as Jigsaw."

We looked at each other for a few moments before she said, "Yes. I gave her the address. I have no idea if she was successful in her endeavour."

She didn't approve of the change in policy. I could tell by the way she held herself, stiff and inflexible. But rules were rules and so she'd complied.

I thanked her and left her office with the address of John and Adele Preston and their son, Benjamin, in my hand.

21

"I gave away all his stuff."

Simon James lived on Christine Avenue at the northernmost part of Burleigh Heads that bordered Miami Beach. The report he'd made of his missing son was in the first file I opened when I was sitting in the fan-forced oven of my car at 2 o'clock that afternoon. His son, William James, had gone missing five years ago when he was eleven years old.

"Even if he *did* come back, he'd have outgrown it all by now," he said. "I've got a few things here if he wants them. You can take them to him if you like. Is he in jail?"

"No sir, he isn't."

I didn't want to tell him about the bodies found at Tamborine Mountain until I was sure that one of them was his child. All I had at this stage was a suspicion. A good one, but still only a suspicion. The last thing he needed was to be told his son had been murdered and then, at a time in the future, be told that we'd made a terrible mistake and his son was doing well and pumping gas in Adelaide, not dead and buried in a mountain grave with five other boys.

He nodded and smiled a sad smile, happy to hear what I told him. "That's good. That's good. I hoped he'd be okay."

He walked over to a side table and opened a drawer. "Got these report cards here." He pulled them out as if they had been placed there only yesterday. "Kept them all these years."

He walked back over to me and handed them to me.

"Not much to report but he always worked hard."

"Did he take anything when he left?"

He nodded. "A backpack with a change of clothes and a picture of his mother." He pointed to a picture frame featuring a pretty woman smiling widely up at the camera. "I replaced it with this one when he took the original one with him."

He stared at the frame lost in his own thoughts for a few moments and I didn't have the heart to interrupt. In the back of my mind was the decaying photograph of a woman sitting in the lab that had been found in the backpack of one of the bodies at the gravesite.

"She died a year before he left, and Billy took it hard." His voice choked off and I could see him trying to swallow. "Excuse me. I can't talk about it for too long."

"Take your time, sir," I said.

"I got home that day and he wasn't home. I didn't think much of it at the time. I'd enrolled him in a class during the school holidays because I couldn't get time off work to be with him but more and more, he wasn't turning up at all at the classes, just playing hooky. But when he wasn't home by 6 o' clock, I really started getting worried."

"Do you have any idea of where he would go?"

He shook his head. "I never knew. He just liked to go off somewhere by himself." He looked over at the frame again. "Always took the picture with him."

He gulped again. "I called the police and they told me they'd keep an eye out for him and that I should come in to the station in the morning and make a missing person's report if he didn't come home by then." He sighed. "He didn't come home so I went in and filled out the report."

He looked up at me. "It was all my fault this happened. I was always working. I should have been here for him after his mother died. But it was so hard, you know? I still had to pay the bills and put food on the table."

"You shouldn't blame yourself for what happened, sir. It wasn't your fault. That's just not true. Sometimes, when kids get things into their heads, there's no way of getting it out again."

He looked at me hard. "There's something you're not telling me." His eyes searched my face. "He's dead, isn't he?"

For a cop, this is just about the worst moment in the world. You know that you should tell the truth and let the family move on but you also know that what you're going to say is going to hurt even more than their not knowing at all.

I nodded slowly. "We can't be sure, sir, but we found the remains of a buried child. There was a backpack with a spare set of clothes in it and a picture of what could be a woman."

He dropped his head and began to cry softly.

"For years, I believed he was alive. I felt it," he placed his hand over his heart, "here. I knew what the feeling was. You want to believe so badly, that your brain arranges for you to actually see it. I used to dream that one day he'd show up at the door. The bell would ring and there he'd be, looking just fine. It was my lifeline and any lifeline is better than none." He sighed deeply. "But lately, somehow, I knew." He looked up at me, his eyes red and shining. "I knew."

His face was a pool of sadness as he stared out of the window. "Do you have a child, Sergeant?"

"Yes, I do."

"Then you know that you never stop worrying. Never. You remember the first time he climbed out of his cot and fell to the floor before you could reach him. When he grows older and rides his bike and climbs trees and walks to school on his own and darts out in front of cars instead of waiting for the light to change, you try to pretend it's okay. You say, 'That's kids. I did the same at his age.' But always in the back of your throat is this scream, *Don't. Stop.*" He turned from the window and looked at me. "It never goes away. The worry and the fear. Not for even for one second."

I remembered the time Jazz fell off a swing when she was at the top of the loop. I'd heard the crack as her head hit the ground and for a while, she lay motionless until I got to her and I thought she was dead. Just for a second, but I remember the horror of that thought until she opened her eyes and began crying. Nothing could compare to the pain this man was feeling.

"We may need you to come down to the station to see if you can identify the backpack and the photo. Just to be sure. It's deteriorated a lot as you can imagine and so has the picture but you may be able to recognise it. Will you be up to that sometime soon?"

He nodded.

I stood, preparing to leave. "If there is anything I can do, just let me know, sir."

"Thank you, Sergeant. I will."

22

The next file said Sonya Bennett was the grandmother of Jason Bennett, another child who'd been reported missing. She lived in Mermaid Beach, a neighbourhood north of Burleigh Heads and Miami Beach that wasn't quite up to their standards but was lined with nicely kept homes and duplexes.

Ms Bennett's home was a second-floor duplex. A tall overweight, grey-haired woman answered the door after I knocked. She gave me the impression of self-sufficiency and competence and I instinctually knew that she would make a good witness if ever one was needed.

"Ms Bennett?"

"Yes?"

"My name is Sergeant Curtis of Surfers Paradise Police Station. May I come in and talk to you for a moment please."

Her hand moved to her throat as she stood aside for me to enter.

"You're here about Jason, aren't you?" she asked.

"Yes, ma'am. You filed a missing person's report on Jason a year ago. Is that correct?"

She sighed deeply and as I watched her face, visions of the last victim floated before my eyes with horrible clarity.

"Yes. That is correct."

"Do you have a picture of your grandson, ma'am?"

She walked over to a cabinet where a row of silver-framed photos were displayed. She chose two and turned around before handing them both to me. One frame contained a photo of a boy sitting on the lap of a teenage girl. Both were smiling at the camera, the kind of smile where you have been *told* to smile – a stretched smile full of teeth.

"Was Jason living with you when he disappeared last year?"

"He'd been living with me for several years." The skin around her eyes grew tight with embarrassment. "My daughter decided she wanted to see the world and a baby just wasn't in her picture of things. She told me she wanted to leave him with me until she came back for him. She hasn't called me since she left five years ago."

"Can you tell me about the day Jason disappeared?"

She nodded and seemed to compose her thoughts before beginning.

"January 2nd last year. He left the house at 9.00 o'clock that morning to go to a friend's house where his parents were going to take both the boys to their religious class. At 5.00 pm, when he hadn't returned home, I rang their house to see if he was on his way home but the boy's parents said that he hadn't been there at all that day. When Jason hadn't turned up at their house by 9.30 am, they assumed he was making his own way to the church so they took their son to his religious class alone. I looked in his room and a backpack was missing."

I looked down at the second photo. The boy was wearing a black t-shirt with Metallica printed in decorative Old English type across the top.

"This shirt," I asked as I leaned forward for her to see. "Was he wearing that shirt when he disappeared?"

"Yes, that's right. It was his favourite. Those jeans as well."

In my mind, I saw the small body lying face down in his makeshift grave. I saw the black t-shirt and the jeans covering the body that was part skeleton and part waxwork figure and I felt sorry for the woman standing before me who would have to come in and identify it as her grandchild.

"If he wasn't at his friend's house that day, do you have any idea where he could have gone?"

She shook her head. "He liked to be alone. He was always going off somewhere on his own. He was a difficult child. He needed a lot of attention and it fell to me because my daughter never really wanted to be a mother. When she left, all she left for him was a note under his pillow." She shook her head sadly and her eyes showed a pain I wished I hadn't seen.

"Did he ever say anything about trying to find her?" I asked.

"No. Even though he was always very interested in what she looked like, he never really said much about anything." She shrugged. "He was only four years old when she left. A couple of years later, he began to ask a few questions about her. I told him what she was like when she was his age and all the things that he did that reminded me of her. He seemed interested for a while but the questions stopped and I didn't want to hurt him anymore than he probably already was." Her mouth hardened until white dots appeared at either corner. "We dealt with it as best we could."

With a nod of her head, she indicated the photo. "That's the only recent photo I have of her."

"What school did Jason go to, Ms Bennett?"

"Mermaid State School, just around the corner."

"Do you mind if I have a look in his room?"

She stood up and said, "Not at all."

I stepped into what had been Jason's room and, in a way, still was. Young boy's furniture sat frozen in time. Books and model cars, posters of bands and bikes. All like a portal to the past revealing bits of a life that accumulate in the shadows of a missing child's room. The wardrobe showed clothes hung neatly on hangers and on the shelf above the hanging space, a Playstation and three games sat patiently waiting to be used again. There were no board games like Monopoly and Scrabble to help fill the void. No games that a young boy would play with a couple of his friends.

I could feel her standing in the doorway, almost as if she didn't want to enter. I could feel her keeping her distance as if she couldn't quite bring herself to walk into the room.

Drawers of a dressing table held basketball cards held tightly together with a rubber band as well as school photos and school reports, almost as if she was simply minding them for him until he came back home again. I picked up a school report and glanced down at the grades.

"Doesn't look like much, I know," she said, indicating the reports. "He tried hard but only managed to get C's. I used to tell him that trying was all I expected of him. The grades didn't matter as long as he tried."

A strange 'something' had been buzzing and ticking in the back of my brain, loudly, and it felt like the melody of a song I was trying to remember while the radio played a completely different tune. In the past five minutes, she'd given me some piece of information and my subconscious had absorbed it and was sending off signals. But for the life of me, I had no idea of what it was. It was just this *feeling* that I'd overlooked something she'd said, and I really should have taken notice.

I have always taken advantage of these thoughts and impressions. I turned around and took one last look at the room. There was nothing here that shouldn't be here but the feeling persisted.

"After all this time, why have they sent you to come and look at his room and talk to me?" she asked, dragging me away from my thoughts. "A policeman did all this twelve months ago. Every time I rang, they said there was no further information they could give me." Her eyes travelled over my face and her eyes held so much pain. "You've found him, haven't you?"

I couldn't put it off any longer. "We think so. Yes, ma'am. I'm sorry." I didn't need to say anything else. Two simple words, I'm sorry, and she knew the terrible truth.

Her hands flew to her mouth and her eyes widened and glistened with unshed tears. "Oh no. No."

She spun around and I could see her visibly trying to pull herself together. Her shoulders heaved for a few seconds and then suddenly, her back straightened and she pulled her shoulders back before she turned to face me again.

Her chin still trembled but her voice was steady. "I want to see him. I *have* to see him."

I'd seen this before. Parents who needed proof that their child had died. Parents who thought they were strong enough to view their child in the last terrible moments of their lives. And I'd seen the look of shock every time. It wasn't something I looked forward to but it was part of my job to support them as they tried to comprehend the evil that was a part of this world.

I nodded. "We'll need you to identify the body and the backpack we found with him. But I need to warn you, he's been dead for the whole year and it will be very painful for you to see." I watched her chin tremble. "Is there someone you'd like to come with you? A friend or a relative?"

She shook her head and made an attempt to steady herself. "Jason was all I had. My life." Her chin began to tremble again.

"I'm sorry, Sergeant." Her voice trembled as she spoke. "When a tragedy like this hits you - when it first hits you - it's the end of the world. It's like being dumped in the ocean during a storm. The water tosses you and thrashes you and there is nothing you can do but try to stay afloat. Part of you, even most of you, doesn't even want to keep your head above water. You want to stop fighting and just sink away. But you can't. The survival instinct won't let you. Either way, like it or not, you stay afloat. But you see, after a while, the storm part is over. And that's when it gets even worse. I guess you can say you're washed ashore. But all that thrashing and tossing causes irreparable harm. You are in tremendous pain and that's still not the end of it. Because now you're left with an awful alternative."

I waited while she struggled with her emotions.

"You try to move past the pain. You try to get on with your life." She closed her eyes and shook her head firmly. "But you never forget. Forgetting is too obscene."

"I can only imagine what it must be like," I said.

She looked at me. "You don't feel like a normal person anymore. You lose a child and from that moment on, you feel isolated from everyone else. You can't help it but you hang on to your pain. All you can hope is that he's alright and that he's safe. Deep in your heart, you know the truth but you just can't face it." She took a deep breath. "I want you to promise you'll catch this killer."

"I want to catch him as much as you do, and I promise you, I won't rest until I *do* find him."

She wiped a tear away from her cheek. "I can't tell you how much it hurts. I sit in this room and I don't know what to do. What angers me now is that this man is out there on the streets right now, having a good time while my grandchild is dead. He'll get himself a lawyer who'll say this killer is insane. If he doesn't go to jail, he'll go to some institution for the criminally insane and he'll be out in no time at all, rehabilitated." She snorted the last word contemptuously. "He'll get three meals a day and the clothes on his back. What's not fair is that he'll be alive and my Jason is dead."

Her tone throughout was matter-of-fact, and the dark-eyed look she gave me seemed all more painful because of it.

"I want this man punished," she continued. "I want to know why he did it and I want to tell him face-to-face exactly what he did to my life the day he took Jason's."

There's a certain look a parent gets when she's feeling protective for her child and it's an animal look. The danger that streams off it is almost palpable. It's not something that can be reasoned with, and even though it stems from the depths of love, it knows no pity or boundaries. As I looked into her eyes, she had that look.

"I can't promise you that you'll get that opportunity," I said as I took hold of her hand. "But rest assured, I'll tell him for you."

I knew she was trying to harden herself against the pain. It's better to get mad than to go on feeling heartsick and defenceless. That's the long and the short of it.

I held her hand for a second longer and let loose a breath. "Let me know when you plan to come in and identify the body. I'll stay with you."

She nodded absently and I excused myself, leaving her to grieve in the silence of her grandson's room.

I'm going to get you I said to myself as I put the car in gear and headed back to the station.

23

As soon as I entered the squad room, I pulled a laminated A4 sheet that had the extension numbers of different departments from my top drawer and at the same time pulled the phone over in front of me. I wanted to talk to Walt Mason. I found the number and dialled. As the phone rang, I checked my watch. Almost 4 o'clock.

"Come on. Come on," I whispered. "Answer the damn phone."

On the tenth ring, he picked up the phone.

"What?"

"Did I catch you at a bad time?" I asked. "Or haven't you done the 'Phone Manners' module in your job manual yet."

"Curtis, is that you?" he asked with exasperation in his voice. "Again?"

"Right first time. How are you, Walt?"

"How am I? HOW AM I?" His voice got louder with the second question. "How the hell do I sound?"

"Charming," I said.

I could hear him sigh. "This had better be good. I was just leaving and I'm already late. If I don't get home on time tonight I'll miss Jenny's band recital and my wife will never let me forget it. I promised I'd be home for once so this had better be good."

"I'm ringing to see if you've managed to look at the body of Joey Caruthers yet."

"I just finished. You'll get the report in the morning."

I let the words hang without saying anything. I wanted the report tonight but I wasn't sure how I was going to get it, given Walt's present frame of mind.

I heard a sigh in the silence over the phone, then Walt said resignedly, "Okay, Jack. He died on site *after* being tossed into the bush."

My heart skipped a beat. "After? How can you tell?"

"Are you questioning my skills, Jack?"

"Are we being a little sensitive, Walt?"

"You do my job while being surrounded by dead kids as far as the eye can see and see how sensitive you become."

There was silence again over the phone. I had nothing to say to that one.

His voice came back again, quieter this time. "Lividity is how I know. Lividity is what happens to a person's blood after death. The heart stops, blood pressure collapses, liquid blood drains and settles into the lowest part of the body under simple gravity. It stays there and over a period of time it stains the skin purple. Somewhere between three and six hours later the colour starts to fix and then it fixes permanently, like a developed photograph. A guy who falls down dead on his back will have a pale chest and a purple back. Vice versa for a guy who falls down dead on his front. This kid showed major fixed lividity on his front consistent with him dying facedown. If he'd died elsewhere and carried to the bush in, say, the trunk of a car, he would have shown signs of early lividity on his side or back and then fixed lividity on his front. There's no sign of that."

I didn't want to say the words but they had to be said. I took a deep breath and asked, "Was he raped?"

"No signs of forced penetration which means no rape."

"Thank God for that," I breathed. "What's the time of death?"

The sigh I heard meant I was already pushing the limit. "Around twenty to twenty-four hours prior to the discovery of the body. On the first day after death," Mason continued, "flies lay their eggs in the moist, dark places such as the nose, mouth eyelids, rectum. They tell us a lot. A few days later, I'd expect to see maggots and flies all over the body. An entomologist can take pupae from the body and fix the time of death according to the different stages of putrefaction. The length of putrefaction determines when infestation first took place and gives us the approximate time of death. Eggs had been laid in this boy's body but none had hatched yet," he said, "which would make it less than twenty-four hours but more than twenty."

I heard another sigh through the earpiece. "There's something else, isn't there?" I asked.

"Yes," he said. "We have anti-mort abrasions. Most wounds have four stages of healing. Scabbing. The formation of epithelial, which is the tissue that forms on the superficial part of the skin and lines the blood vessels. Thirdly, regeneration hyperplasia where there is an increase in the number of normal cells and lastly, the formation of granulation tissue. This new tissue forms across the wound to provide a framework that supports the epithelial cells that migrate into the open area and fill it. The newly formed granulation tissue also secretes a fluid that kills bacteria."

"Wow," was all I could say. "You even sound like you know what you're talking about."

"Okay, okay. What I'm trying to say is that these scrapes were at the second stage which means his body went through four to six hours of healing before he died."

"He was alive for up to six hours on the mountain before he died?" I asked incredulously. "Is that what you're saying?"

"That's what I'm saying."

There was a deep silence over the phone while I digested this new piece of horrific information.

"What was the cause of death?" I asked.

"Now here's where it gets interesting. We did a test on his stomach contents and found it contained half-digested meats, vegetables and cheese consistent with having eaten pizza a couple of hours before death. Not just that, it contained huge amounts of trichloroethylene, otherwise known as methyl trichloride."

"Translated that means?"

"Chloroform. Pure and simple."

I switched my phone to the other ear and pulled my notepad over while I jotted this new information down.

"I thought chloroform was an anaesthetic that you breathed in prior to an operation," I stated.

"It is, although medicine has advanced in the past few years. Chloroform can cause vomiting and after an operation, that's the last thing you need. They use ether these days with better post-operative effects. But getting back to chloroform. You can also ingest it with food. The boy probably didn't even know what he was eating. It's a colourless liquid with a pleasant non-irritating odour and a slightly sweet taste. It was unlucky for the killer that the boy was found so soon after death because tests are only useful for a short time after you've been exposed to it. Another day or so and we still wouldn't know what killed the boy. Unlucky for the killer but lucky for us. He probably killed the other boys the same way but there'll never be any way to tell."

"Are you telling me that you can walk into a chemist and buy chloroform over the counter?"

"No, not a chemist. Easier than that. A hardware store. Chloroform is also a grease solvent used by a lot of dry cleaners. You can also find it in some paint strippers."

"Jesus," I muttered. "So he overdosed the kids on chloroform? What would the symptoms be?"

"Apparently chloroform affects the central nervous system, the cardiovascular system, stomach, liver and kidneys. Hang on a sec. I've been reading up on it on Google and printed something off." The phone banged loudly as he dropped it on the desk. I heard a rustle of paper over the phone and a muffled "Here it is" before he picked the phone up again. "In the late 1950's, factory workers in the United States who worked to manufacture lozenges were treated for chloroform vapours exposure. Workers reported symptoms of fatigue, a dull-wittedness along with depression and gastrointestinal distress. And that was an extremely mild dose. Chloroform causes relaxation of the bronchial muscle resulting in airway constriction. It can also cause the tongue to fall posteriorly, which will again aid in obstruction of the airway to the lungs. Put that with the paradoxical fear these kids must have felt and you'd have a dead kid in a very short time.'

"What do you mean by paradoxical fear?"

"Fear typically elicits sympathetic responses but in the case of paradoxical fear, there is massive activation of the parasympathetic division. This fear occurs when someone is backed into a corner where there is no escape route or no way to win. The body responds with a decreased heart rate, constriction of the pupils and decreased diameter of the airways or bronchoconstriction. Add that to the effect of chloroform and you have one heartless bastard to contend with."

"Okay," I said tiredly. It wasn't going to be as easy to trace as I'd hoped. "Just send me the report in the morning." As an afterthought, I added, "Thanks for doing it so fast, by the way."

"Just do me a favour, Jack."

"What do you want? I owe you a few."

"Stay in the squad room and don't leave it. Every time you go outside, *I* end up with another dead child on my table."

24

The address Children's Services had given me was for John and Adele Preston at a house on the outskirts of Ashmore. Before heading off to see them, I decided to call first to make sure that someone would be at home. I checked for the phone number in the phone book but found no listings for any Preston's at Ashmore. I tried Queensland Transport and again came up with nothing. It looked like they'd either moved out of Queensland or neither of them drove a motor vehicle. Next I tried The Department of Family Services to see if any payments were being made to either of the Prestons and I hit pay dirt. Money had been regularly paid into the account of John Preston listed as living at The Rose Garden Cottage for the past ten years for the care of a Benjamin Preston.

I knew where The Rose Garden Cottage was without having to look at a street directory. I knew it very well. It was a rooming house for single men only a couple of streets past Caville Avenue in downtown Surfers Paradise and close to the police station. It was in the same area as the strip joints, sleazy no-frills bars and tourist traps but there were very few 'rose gardens' in the area, if any, that I could remember.

I called Sam over and filled her in on the information from Children's Services. When I finished, I said, "I've found Peter Ashton's adoptive father. The address comes up as The Rose Garden Cottage."

She raised her eyebrow a notch. "So, what now? Are you going over there to see him?" she asked.

"We both are. This time I want someone with me because to tell the truth, I can't trust myself to stay calm and collected while I speak to this animal." I stood up and grabbed my coat. "Come on, let's walk. It just a few blocks. I could use the fresh air and we can talk along the way."

We headed off, settling into a slow sort of half-speed gait. I used short paces to help Sam keep up with me and I felt pretty stupid doing it. I must have looked like a penguin.

"How'd the interview with Ashton go?" Sam asked as we walked.

"I got through without pulling out my gun."

She raised her eyebrows. "It's a good thing we're not in private enterprise and depending on you to sweet-talk the customers."

"I gave him my charming smile, my Tom Cruise, if you must know. Sadly, it didn't impress him."

"No class," she replied with a smirk.

We passed a shop with a poster of a girl in thigh-high black boots and minuscule string-bikini bottoms and nothing else, stuck to the front window. She had forgotten to put on a top and she had a finger in her mouth and a look on her face that could not be confused with anything else in the world. A sign told me her name was Candy Wrapping and that she had 'More inside.'

I can never understand how people like this kind of sleaze. It made me want to have a shower and a shot of penicillin. In my view, perversion is so dirty, it's depressing. It had to weigh you down. Don't get me wrong. I'm a guy and I have urges like any other man but I've never been able to understand how anyone could confuse filth with eroticism.

Of late, the city has been doing a clean-up, and in a sense, it's made my job easier. The St Vincent de Paul van now knows where to cruise. The runaways and homeless are in the open now and more obvious. But the homeless are not always pretty. They vomit. They soil themselves because they often can't find toilets. Enough said. You can sit on one of the prettiest streets in the country and if you've been sitting long enough, you begin to see the ugliness.

Sadly, St Vinnies loses a lot of kids, more than they save. And you can forget the 'syphoning out the weeds' analogy. It's stupid because it implies that we're getting rid of something bad and preserving something good. In fact, it's just the opposite. Try this one instead: the street is more like a cancer. Early screening and preventive treatment is the key to long-term survival. Not much better, but you have the idea. I know St Vinnies turns lives around but I also know that what happens here on the streets, in what can be called a cesspool, never leaves these people. The damage has already been done. The people from St Vinnies try to work around it and they may even help kids to go on. But a lot of times, the damage is permanent.

The good part about the clean-up is the residents and tourists are no longer subjected to blacked-out windows reading ADULTS ONLY or worse still, signs that read like SHAVING RYAN'S PRIVATES. In actual fact, the city itself wasn't cleaner, it just *looked* cleaner. But sleaze like this never really dies. Sleaze is like a cockroach. It survives by burrowing and hiding and I don't think you can kill it.

There are negatives to hiding the sleaze. When sleaze is obvious, you can scoff and fell superior. People need that. It's an outlet for some. Another advantage to in-the-open sleaze is the question: what would you prefer: an obvious frontal assault or a snakelike danger hiding in the long grass? Finally, and maybe I'm looking at this too closely, you can't have a front without a back. You can't have an up without a down. You can't have light without dark, good without evil or purity without sleaze.

I hesitated before moving on. "I wonder what they're selling," I muttered.

"Doesn't matter," Sam said. "Even if you wanted it, you can't afford it."

Even as we spoke, a fiftyish-looking guy came out of the darkness inside and stood in the doorway. He looked me up and down slowly as if he disapproved of my looks. He looked worse for wear, but then again, I bet he hadn't started out too sparkly in the first place. His hair was eighties and Aeorosmith-long, parted in the middle and on the greasy side. The patches of skin visible under the beard were pockmarked. His jeans looked like they'd been trampled by a pack of dingoes and the waist was too big, giving him that ever-desirable plumber-butt-plunge look. A pack of Marlboros was rolled up in his sleeve like something from a tacky seventies James Dean movie.

"Shows about to start," he said through nicotine-stained teeth.

"Sorry I can't stay for it," I replied.

Just ahead of us, two boys in their early teens turned the corner on Rollerblades, their feet slashing expertly back and forth in front of each other, bodies low, arms swinging in tandem with their feet. They passed by us, one on either side as Sam and I moved closer together. They laughed as they nearly clipped me.

I turned back and glared, which they found even funnier, and then I lapsed into a kind of autopilot mode as the ground blurred beneath me and my mind drifted to my present state of singleness.

I turned to Sam. "If I wanted to ask you out, how would I go about it?"

Her head snapped to face me and she smiled. "What? You going to give me a go after you've finished with the poster girl? I'll have to see if my husband can baby sit so give me a little notice, okay?"

"No really. If I met you in a bar how would I go about asking you out? Do I ask for your mobile number or do I give you mine? What?"

"Okay," she said. "If it were me?"

I nodded.

"I'd give you my mobile number."

I put my hand over my heart and smiled. "Wow!" We walked a few paces before I said, "You know I'd never call you."

She turned to me with an amazed look on her face. "Well, thanks a lot! That's really humiliating. I give you my number and," she shrugged, "nothing?"

"Well, you see, you scare me a little."

She made a snorting noise through her nose and shook her head.

"Don't get me wrong," I said. "You'd get a lot of hang-ups but I could never actually speak to you." She punched me good-naturedly on the arm and grinned.

The Rose Garden Cottage came into view and a man stood leaning against the doorjamb with his arms folded across his chest like a chubby version of Sinatra leaning against a lamppost with a cigarette in his hand.

He looked like someone who was stuck in the 60's. His hair was greying and slicked back and his skin had a pale nightclub pallor.

We walked up the front stairs towards him and he didn't move an inch. He just eyed us both up and down.

"Can you tell us if John Preston lives here?" I asked.

His cigarette paused halfway to his mouth, the smoke curling like a white snake as he squinted at me through it. I'd seen guys like him picking cigarette butts out of ashtrays in hotel lobbies.

"Who wants to know?" he growled.

I made a show of pulling out my badge and said, "Sergeant Curtis, Surfers Paradise Police." I tilted my head to Sam. "This is Detective Neil. Now stop thinking like a tree stump and just answer the question."

He tried to stare me down, took a slow drag on his cigarette and breathed the smoke out through his nose, then jerked his head towards the inside of the house.

"Room 3. Ground floor near the back."

It was only as we passed him that I noticed the smell. He smelt like a cigarette out for a breath of fresh air. I heard him mutter, "You're welcome," but I didn't break my stride.

Room 3 was the last door on the left down a dark corridor that had seen its last paint job in the 80s. I couldn't see them but I heard the crackle of cockroaches scampering away from our feet.

Sam planted her feet firmly on the ground and stood sideways to the door. She raised her left arm and hit the door hard with the fleshy side of her hand. She waited a few seconds and hit it again, only this time harder and announcing "POLICE". Then she stepped back.

"You know," I leaned in to talk, "I'd say the guy is there is relieved to hear it's just the police after that knock. At least he knows it's not an earthquake."

The man who opened the door was blondish but it obviously came from a bottle or what little there was left of it. His day-old whiskers shone white in the hallway light and his nose was swollen by time and alcohol and pinched by a pair of thick ill-fitting glasses. He was wearing a beltless dressing gown with permanent stains under the arms and boxer shorts exposing legs like skinny stilts. He gaped at me myopically through dirty glasses while a cigarette balanced precariously from behind one ear. The gloom had dulled his eyes to a pale blue and fed his pallor deepening the red blotches on his face. His skin tone said 'indoors': chalky white. Beside him, I looked glowing with good health.

"Who the hell are you?" he asked, clicking his false teeth together when he spoke.

This is what comes from watching too many cop shows. Everyone has an attitude and everyone thinks they're saying something original and making a point.

Again I pulled out my badge and introduced Sam.

"Can we talk to you for a few moments?"

"What about?" he asked, glancing from me to Sam and back to me again, still shielding himself behind the door.

Over my shoulder, the guy was still standing there trying to look like he wasn't listening.

"I'd rather talk about this privately if I may."

He grudgingly let us in, thankfully pulling his robe tightly around his body and tying it with the belt before shutting the door.

Two things hit me at once. Firstly, the dark. The only light was a low-watt bulb hanging from the centre of the ceiling. Secondly, the smell. Take your most vivid memory of fresh air and the great outdoors and then imagine the exact opposite. The stuffiness almost made me afraid to inhale. I wondered when the last time a window had been opened and I could imagine never.

As my eyes began to adjust, I looked at him and knew that a man like him would never be given a normal job. There was no single explanation I could think of except everything seemed a bit askew. I thought of the way drunk people pretend to be sober, the way they might get all the details right but fool nobody. John Preston was imitating a normal, socialised member of the public but not quite accomplishing it. His dressing gown was slightly too big and he had rolled one sleeve inwards and the other outwards. His belt had apparently split because it was wound about with masking tape. Days ago, when he *had* shaved, he had missed an improbably large section under his jaw.

The room was sparsely furnished. There was only an unmade bed with a knocked about dressing table near a window, a small round table with an empty Chicken McNugget box and a squashed packet of cigarettes on top and two wooden chairs. Under the table was a stack of newspapers and on top of them was a bottle of Seven Pipers Scotch and a dirty glass. The floor was littered with tobacco. A television stood on a small stand and an old threadbare recliner sat within kissing distance of it. And that was it. I didn't know if he was a psychopath or not but I certainly knew that he lived alone. There was definitely no longer a *Mrs* Preston to add the feminine touches.

I sometimes think that the most important words anybody can say to us is not *'I love you'* but *'You can't go out looking like that.'* People say it to us over and over again when we're children and most of us internalise it and say it to ourselves and loved ones when we're adults. We grow up learning to do the sort of things other people do, to say the sort of things other people say, so that we can pass unnoticed in the world. Then there are men like John Preston who will probably never have anyone to say those words to him ever again. Looking at him made me think of my own sorry situation and I hoped like hell that I wasn't seeing a vision of myself in twenty years time.

He heaved the recliner around and motioned for Sam to sit down. She hesitated then sat down gingerly while he sat down on one high-backed wooden chair and I occupied the other one. He bent down and retrieved a disposable lighter from the floor and took the cigarette from behind his ear and lit it up nervously. We all looked uncomfortable, like mismatched chess pieces in a live game.

"What do you want?" As he blew smoke out through his nose, I wondered if it was my imagination or if it was evasiveness that I detected.

"We've come to ask you about the boy you and your wife adopted twenty years ago."

Preston stopped moving. There wasn't so much as a blink but I could make out the sharp intake of his breathing as he exhaled through his nostrils. He stared at me for a long moment, his mouth coming open and exposing his yellowed teeth.

"Benny?" he finally said. "You're here about Benny? That's a joke, right? My wife and him left me ten years ago. Emptied out the bank account and left. Took everything I owned and left me broke. I had to move here and live like this." He waved a hand around to emphasise what he was left with.

"And you've not seen them since?" I asked. I glanced over at Sam who was perched on the edge of the chair as if at any moment she would jump off and head for the door.

"You were still collecting money from Children's Services though." I tried to keep the edge out of my voice. "Did you keep the money if you didn't know where they were? That's an offence, Mr Preston."

His face turned red. "I told the Children's Services about it but nobody listened," he said. "That's what the trouble is these days. Nobody ever listens. You say something and they don't hear you because they think you're scum or something."

He looked down at my hands clasped together between my legs. "Shouldn't you be writing all this down, or something?"

"I won't forget any of this." My grin must have resembled the wolf from the 'Little Red Riding Hood' story. All teeth and charm. "Trust me on that one."

He squinted his eyes at me but then shrugged and settled back a little in his chair, waiting for me to continue.

"You say you *told* Children's Services but nobody listened to you?" I asked.

"Nobody," he answered. "Not ever. I told them Adele left with the boy and they said that it wasn't their responsibility anymore. He had been legally adopted to both of us and if she took him off with her, then there was nothing they could do. He still had a legal parent."

A column of ash crumbled on to his dressing gown and he ground the cigarette out in an already overflowing ashtray sitting on the table.

His tone became cloyingly sentimental. "She never cared anyway. Didn't even call me and tell me where she was. I don't even know if she's alive." Just as suddenly, his tone changed. "Wouldn't have her back now if she showed up, though. That'll teach her."

"Do you have any photos of your wife and the boy?" I asked.

"I told you. She took the lot. Left me with just my clothes."

"What about your friends? Did any of them hear from her?"

"Never had any to speak of," he mumbled as he lit another cigarette. "Why're you asking all these questions anyway?" he asked, tilting his head back and blowing smoke towards the already grimy ceiling. "She done something wrong?" There was a stillness to his body that hadn't been there a minute before.

"We've found Benjamin."

Preston's eyes dropped from mine and seemed to leave the room as he studied a far-off memory. In his look was knowledge. I saw it. Instinct told me that what I was going to tell him next he would already know. I glanced over to Sam to see if she'd see it too and she gave a single nod.

I looked back at John Preston.

"You don't seem very excited for a father who hasn't seen his son for more than ten years," I said.

Preston didn't study me so much as stare through me, as if what he was seeing was on the other side of my head. "I guess I'm not surprised because I know he's dead."

I studied him for a long moment, holding my breath in my lungs. "Now why would you say that?" I finally asked. "What would make you think that?"

"Because I know. I've known all along."

"What have you known?"

"That he wasn't coming back." His gaze shifted, tracking the dust motes settling through the air. "He would'a come back if he could've."

This wasn't going the way of any of the scenarios I'd imagined. I had to steer things around to what had happened to the boy.

"When the boy was with you, did you ever hit him?"

I saw his eyes widen but he didn't answer.

"How did you discipline him?" I asked.

His eyes twitched as he plucked at his dressing gown with his free hand. His right leg began jerking up and down, the ball of his foot on the ground and his heel bouncing. He reached over and put another cigarette in his mouth then lit it, leaving it there when he spoke. His face had grown ruddy and the veins in his neck stuck out like cables.

"What the hell are you saying? That I hurt my boy? I did what any parent would do. I clipped him whenever he needed it."

I tried not to look at the spittle that was running down the corner of his mouth and heading towards his chin.

"We have hospital records that say he had several serious injuries up to the age of ten." I tried to keep the emotion out of my voice and as a result, my voice sounded strained.

He stood up and began pacing the room. "He was clumsy, is all. He had this leg that gave him trouble and he fell down a lot. Always falling, he was."

"What about your wife? Did she ever hit him?"

He stopped pacing and turned to face me, a strange look on his face. Sometimes you meet a person whose innate goodness bursts at you with an almost blinding light. And then sometimes, you meet the exact opposite – someone whose very presence smothers you with a heavy cloak of decay.

Something slimy and – forgive me, but there is no other word I can find to express this feeling – something *evil* flitted across his face. The look was so fleeting, it was there one second and gone the next. It disappeared as quickly as it came. He leant forward in his chair and began to speak earnestly to me.

"Yeah," he said slowly as he sat back down again. "She was real tough on him, sometimes couldn't control him. Used to back-answer her and she wouldn't stand for it. Used to hit him with anything she had in her hand. Had a temper that one. I remember her coming home from work that last day and he was in his room when he should have been at classes. She got real mad. We paid good money for that class, she yelled at him. Money we didn't have. She yelled some more at him and before I knew it, she was hitting him. Knocked him down on the ground, she did."

If that wasn't a bullshit word salad, I don't know what was.

"Didn't you try to stop her?"

He sat back and looked down at the floor.

"Wouldn't have done no good. She'd turn on me then." He took another drag on the cigarette as his eyes flicked up to my face and then back down to the floor again.

I didn't believe his story for a moment. He was displaying classic guilt symptoms. Not being able to maintain eye contact, agitation and the nervous twitch in his leg was really beginning to irritate me.

"That was the last day I saw either of them ever again," he said.

"They left that day? Both of them?"

"Yeah. He was hurt real bad. Banged his head on the table. Bleeding everywhere, he was. She said she was going to take him to the hospital and she left. Never came back."

I tried not to think of the boy cowering and vulnerable while this man beat him to death.

I stared at him for a few moments willing his eyes to meet mine. Wanting him to see the doubt I was feeling. Eventually he did look up but his eyes dropped instantly when he looked into mine.

"But he still went with her when she left? Don't you find that strange, Mr Preston?"

He shrugged and mumbled. "Had no choice, did he?"

I suddenly felt angry. I knew I should act professionally but he irritated me almost to the point of hitting him. "You know what, Preston? I don't believe a word you've told us."

His eyes widened but he said nothing.

"You're slimy and you're a liar and I think you had something to do with Benjamin's death. When I can prove it, trust me I will be back and I'll throw the book at you."

His face had gone a deep red and he spluttered, "You can't talk to me like that! I have rights you know!"

"So did the child you abused, but that didn't stop you from beating him. People like you make me sick."

In my peripheral vision, I could see Sam instantly stand up, ready to leave.

He was still blinking and stuttering with rage when I said, "I'm sure we'll have some more questions for you at a later date so *please* don't leave Surfers for any reason."

We let ourselves out as he leant over to reach for the phone. Outside, I felt like I'd just emerged from the insect house at the zoo. Sam and I began walking and she smirked, "That went well."

I lifted my face towards the sun and let the warm wind gust over it.

"He's definitely hiding the fact that he beat the boy. That wasn't his wife doing that, it was him. But as much as I despise him, I don't think he knew that the boy was dead." I glanced over at Sam. "That's just an instinct and I could be wrong. What about you?"

"I think he's poor, uneducated, lonely, disturbed, self-pitying, vicious and damaged. And he was probably a bully. And yes, as guilty as hell of abusing that boy. I think she left and took the boy with her to stop it."

I nodded. "Certainly looks that way. But if Benjamin *did* die on that day, who buried him in Tamborine Valley?"

"Maybe he died in the car before she got him to the hospital. Maybe she got scared that she'd be charged with the abuse and panicked. I can't see *him*," she jerked her thumb behind her in the direction of the boarding house, "owning up to the abuse. He'd just say *she* was the one who did it like he just did. In any case, she'd be charged with the abuse as well as him."

"Everything you've said is right. But that means it was Preston who killed the other boys." I looked across at Sam. "And I have serious doubts about that. He's a mean, vicious man who constantly abused his son to the point of hospitalisation. But killing other boys and burying them alongside Benjamin? Why would he do that? For one thing, what boy would get into a car with *him* even if he had a car, which he doesn't? Don't forget, we both agreed that these kids had to have trusted the person they went with. I can't see any of the kids trusting *him*? And what was the reason for the killings in any case?"

"He's a serial killer. They have their own agenda," Sam said.

I was shaking my head. "He just doesn't fit the profile. I know there are always exceptions but I can't see him doing the other boys. I'd say yes, he's guilty of Benjamin's abuse and murder but Preston just doesn't have the brains to mastermind the other ones. Which puts us back to where we were before. How do we prove he killed Benjamin and who killed the other boys?"

We walked in silence for a few minutes both lost in our own thoughts.

"When we get back to the station, see if you can come up with an address for Adele Preston," I said. "She's about the only one now who can tell us what actually happened." I checked my watch. 4.30 pm.

"By the time you get that address, it'll be too late to do anything more today."

I glanced over at her. Her eyes were hooded and I could see dark shadows etched on either side of her nose bridge. "It's been a long day. Head off home after you've found it. There's only so much we can do in one day and you need to regroup. I'm going to see Angela Ashton on my way home. I've still got Grayson's voice booming in my head and I want to cover as much ground as I can before he pulls me into his office tomorrow for a review on the case."

"I'm not going to argue with you, Jack. After seeing all of these dead kids, all I want to do is go home and never let mine out of my sight."

25

With the money her father had, Angela Ashton could have been anything she wanted to be, yet she chose to step away from his money and run a modest coffee shop on the main stretch in Surfers Paradise.

The woman who stood by the cash register had ash-brown hair streaked with grey brushed away from her forehead. She was sun-tanned; her lashes bleached white, her eyes brown. Her clothing was conservative: a medium-length brown skirt and a blouse the colour of sand. There wasn't a drop of colour anywhere to be seen.

"Good afternoon. I'm looking for Ms Angela Ashton please?"

Her head tilted to one side in a question.

"I'm Angela Ashton," she said hesitantly. "How may I help you?"

"My name is Sergeant Jack Curtis from Surfers Paradise Police Station. May I speak to you for a moment, please?"

As I spoke, I held out my badge for her to see and she gave me another little frown of puzzlement.

"Is everything alright?" she asked, a tiny frown appearing between her eyes. "My father...?"

"No, your father is fine," I shook my head. "I just need to talk to you about another matter for a moment."

I looked around at the near empty coffee shop. At this time of day, there were few customers. People were heading home to their families, their working day finished.

"Can we sit down?" I asked, gesturing to one of the empty tables.

She looked over to a young waitress cleaning a table and summoned her with her hand.

"Keep an eye on the register for me for a moment please, Melinda. There's no need to counter the money. I'll do that later. Just continue cleaning those tables. When you've finished, you may go home. Thanks. I'll see you tomorrow."

She came around from the back of the counter and as she walked past, I noticed her hair was laced with more silver than I'd first noticed. The look was casual as if she was confident the ageing process didn't concern her at all.

Without asking me to take a seat, she sat down and clenched her hands in her lap. "What can I do for you, Sergeant?"

"This is a delicate question," I began as I sat down opposite her. "I'm sorry I have to ask you this question but you gave birth to a child at Southport Hospital twenty years ago when you were sixteen, is that correct?"

Her expression suggested that she was waiting for the punch line, her half smile beginning to droop. I could see her struggling with a number of conflicting attitudes, most of which were bad.

She looked at me in confusion. Eventually, she nodded slowly.

"You had him adopted?"

She harrumphed in a dismissive way, as if the question was annoying or stupid.

"My *father* had him adopted. But yes, he was adopted." Her mouth curled in a parody of mirth as she said, "Let me hazard a guess here. The adoptive parents think there could be money involved."

"No, absolutely not." I shifted my butt from one side to the other uncomfortably.

"What's this about then?" she asked. "Why come to *me* and talk about this?"

"Well," I started slowly, "You see, there's not too many times that I don't know how to proceed. So, I'll try to do it as painlessly as possible."

A craving for nicotine hit me like a blow. I'd never been a big smoker, just a precious four a day – but the threat of lung cancer had hit home. But right now, a cigarette would have worked magic on my nerves. I didn't relish having to explain the grizzly details to this woman. Even though a woman gives up a child, there is always a bond - a connection - that will always be present. That bond had surfaced with Angela Ashton. She'd made an attempt to find the child eleven years ago and I wasn't sure how this woman would react to my news.

"I'm sorry to have to tell you this but your son, Peter, who was renamed Benjamin by his adoptive parents," I took a deep breath, "has been found buried in a grave on Tamborine Mountain."

A stillness settled over Angela Ashton and I wondered if she had heard me. Like a priest, I've learnt to wait and be receptive to people's emotions and actions. She blinked once slowly, like an owl.

"I'm sorry to have to bring this news to you but we're investigating his murder and it has come up that you tried to contact the adopting parents eleven years ago. Is that also correct?"

She nodded but said nothing. She seemed calm but it was the kind of calm you see in a hospital waiting room.

"Were you successful in your attempt?" I asked.

Angela Ashton watched me as I spoke and her eyes narrowed a little.

"I'd like to know why you'd want to know such a thing."

"During the autopsy, signs of abuse were discovered, serious abuse where he suffered broken limbs over a period of years, and his death was due to injuries that are consistent with child abuse. I'd like to know if you had contact with him because you could then be a witness to this abuse. We don't have a suspect at the moment but an eye witness to this abuse could be the turning point in our case."

Her shoulders slumped. The wrinkles on her face seemed more pronounced now, the crevices sinking deeper into the flesh. She slowly brought one of her hands to her mouth in a fist. She lightly bumped it against her lips as she began talking.

"I did try to contact him but those people wouldn't let me see him. The man, John Preston, said it was too disruptive for a child his age. Peter would have been about nine years old at the time. I rang a few times but....."

She didn't finish. She stared off into the distance silently as car horns sounded and tourists walked past laughing. I waited.

"Ms Ashton?"

"He wouldn't let me," she finished. "I gave him my phone number and asked him, *begged* him, to reconsider. On one occasion, I spoke to his wife and rather surprisingly she was quite nice to me. She said she was sorry but there was nothing she could do about it. Her husband absolutely forbade it."

I let some silence punctuate that. She was talking in a way that hinted she would say more as long as I gave her space. Finally, she began to talk again.

"I left my number with her as well as my address but they never contacted me or allowed me to see my son." Bitterness burned in her voice, even after so many years. She looked into my eyes. "Do you think *they* killed him?"

"We're still in the fact-finding stage here. The indication from your son's remains is that there is a history of chronic physical abuse. I'm sorry to have to tell you that. We're just trying to figure things out."

She went ashen as she stared at me. "Abuse?"

"His remains show trauma." I left it at that. She didn't need to hear the details.

"And what about his funeral. What will happen to his remains?"

I was momentarily taken back by her question.

"Well, I would assume his adoptive parents will be responsible for his burial."

She shook her head. "*I* want to bury my child," she said.

There was an awkward silence for a moment before I replied. In my mind, I saw John Preston and the squalid room he lived in. I was yet to find Adele Preston but I already knew what I would say to the woman in front of me.

"I don't think they'll have too many objections to that after all this time. Benjamin has been dead for ten years."

She squared her shoulders. "Where can I claim his body?" she asked.

"He's still in the morgue at this moment. You'll just need to sign a release form after the body is ready for release." I looked at my watch. "It's too late to contact anyone today but someone will be at the front desk by eight in the morning."

She nodded gently.

I left her sitting alone at the table as I headed out into the foot traffic.

It was shortly before 6 o'clock when I pulled into my garage. It had been a thirteen-hour day with not much to show for it in terms of evidence. Still, I felt satisfied that we were making progress. We had identification of some of the boys and all things would come from that.

26

The criminologists report was easy to read. There were two photos noting the body position and the locality of the physical evidence. The first photo was a picture of the actual site where Joey's body was found and the second was the clearing at the bottom of the gully. I looked around at the sea of faces all waiting for the early morning briefing to start. Sam had been talking on the phone behind a desk by a window and several other detectives had been sitting at their computers when I called them to the meeting. I'd ignored Inspector Grayson's order from two days ago and called a general meeting reasoning that the death of Joey Caruthers and his connection to the other boys had cancelled out his decision to drop the investigation.

A cup of coffee sat by my elbow as I put my glasses on and began to read the report out loud.

"I have here the criminologists report of the last crime scene. Shoe prints size 9 with an estimated body weight of one hundred and fifty pounds were found nearby not matching any of the detectives, medical examiners crew or the hikers."

I looked over the top of my glasses. "You'll note: that makes the killer of average build." I looked back down at the report. "Photographs of the shoe imprint have been sent to the lab for identification of the brand but we're not holding out for much on that. Any tread marks left by any parked vehicle should be ignored since there were several police cars parked in the vicinity. However, one area has appeared to have oil drips and I have authorised castings of those treads. The tyre type has been identified as Bridgestone tyres matching any number of vehicles but most predominantly six cylinder cars such as Fords and Holdens. These particular tyres showed uneven wear on the front tyres, indicating the front end could be out of alignment. When we have a suspect, this could be very important information."

I looked up when I'd come to the end of the report. "Unfortunately, this is the best we can expect. Luck is favouring the murderer right now."

I rubbed my forehead trying to ease the tightness. It was only 9am and I could feel tension between my eyes. "Does anyone remember the Son of Sam, David Berkowitz?"

Most people nodded. "He shot people in parked cars in New York years ago," someone at the back called out.

"That's right," I said. "He just walked up to cars, shot whoever was inside, male or female, then walked away. There was no pattern. There he was, getting away with murder and he felt powerful because of it. This type of killer is called 'random assassin killers' and they're the hardest type of killer to catch because there is no connection to the victims and no way to predict who he might go for next. Most killers kill people they know and that's how they're caught but not so this guy. What we need to do is find out if there *is* any pattern the killer has in finding his victims."

I reached over and picked up the six files I'd placed there ready for the meeting. "Since our the last meeting, I've been down to archives and retrieved all the names and files of missing boys for the last ten years. There were twenty-three."

Someone groaned but no one said anything.

"Something important came out of that." I held up the five files. "I was able to condense it down to these six because of the dates that they all went missing."

As I looked around, everyone's eyes were glued to mine.

"Five of the boys were reported missing on the 2nd January. The same as Joey Caruthers. The exception to this theory is the first boy, Benjamin

Preston. As you all should know by now, Joey Caruthers was the latest victim, making six. But at the time of Joey's murder, the killer didn't know that the other bodies had been found. When he bought Joey to be buried with the others, imagine his shock when he came upon police cars and media surrounding the area. Contingency plans had to be made and the killer would have turned around quickly to escape. But he still had an abducted boy in his car. What was he going to do?"

No one said a word.

"The medical examiner has stated that Joey was dead nearly twenty-four hours when his body was discovered by the hikers on 2nd January. Since Joey was reported missing the same day, it means that the killer didn't wait until nightfall to begin his plan or getting rid of Joey. Sometime, more than likely after lunchtime, he drugged him with lethal dose of chloroform that he'd placed in his food. This would have made Joey very compliant and easy to move as he wouldn't have been able to put up a struggle. Then he went to bury the boy. Joey would have been alive at that time, but only just. The killer was shocked to find the police at his original burial ground and he would have panicked. He turned around and he dumped Joey in the bush on his way down the mountain. He would have known that Joey wouldn't live very long but his plans were disrupted." I looked around. "This could be the turning point for us."

Someone from the back of the room asked, "Because we found his body so soon?"

I nodded. "Not only that but because the killer was forced to react differently from his normal routine. He panicked and that means he could have made a vital mistake. It's up to us to find that mistake."

I took a few deep breaths before continuing. "It's a lazy theory to think that he chooses his victims at random because that's not how this kind of thing is done. Predators take targets of opportunity, yes, but there's always an underlying pattern beneath the victims' selection.

I took a sip of my coffee. It was cold by now but I felt the caffeine in my skin and in my heart.

"So far, all we've been able to find out is that all boys are around the same age and more than likely, some of them, maybe most of them, have been runaways. There is no geographical pattern to the homes of his victims, except that they all lived in reasonably close proximity to Surfers Paradise. That's all. As far as we know, they didn't know each other, didn't go to the same school and they all lived in different suburbs. But there has to be more that connects them than their ages. Something that stopped the crimes being random. Right?"

I looked around. Everyone was nodding and looking at me waiting for me to go on. I could see the interest and speculation in their eyes.

A buzz was beginning to go around the room and I had to call for silence. "Okay, listen up. I went to two homes today, the homes of two of the missing boys. Both boys were loners, both went off on their own regularly and both boys were average scholars. Our next two questions are, *how* did the killer know to pick these kids? And *why* did he?"

As I spoke something shifted in my soul: a feeling that we were getting close and if I could only look at this laterally, the answer would suddenly appear like something from a David Copperfield show.

"This guy is smart, make no mistake about that," I said, "and he knows it. He thinks he is more clever, more intelligent, more cagey than nearly anyone. And that will be his downfall because there is one person who will eventually catch him." I smiled. "Moi."

There were a few snickers around the room and I smiled in return.

"But seriously, this guy somehow manages to lure these boys into his car before he kills them. I want you all to think about that. Why would these kids get into a strange car? Answer is, they trusted him."

I let that question sit in the air for a few seconds. "But why would they trust him?"

I closed my notebook. "There's no rulebook on how to catch this guy. We make it up as we go along and we hope we're doing the right thing. We'll meet back here again tomorrow and hopefully we'll have something concrete by then."

People shuffled away talking to one another as Sam followed me back to my desk.

"How'd it go with Angela Preston last night?" she asked.

"As you'd expect. Shocked but okay." I leaned back on my desk as I spoke. "She said she tried to convince the Prestons to let her see the boy but they refused. I'm not surprised. With the injuries that boy suffered, it would be hard to make up excuses for the bruises and broken body parts."

I rotated my shoulders that were stiffening up from tossing endlessly last night and stretched my back, ignoring the tug in my mid-section.

"By the way, I got Adele Preston's current address yesterday afternoon from the Taxation Department before I went home."

"Good. Does she still live on the Gold Coast or do we have to make sure our passports are up to date?"

Sam smiled. "Sorry. She's still on the Gold Coast."

"Damn. I work much better with a bottle of sunscreen in one hand and a Marguarita in the other."

I grabbed my jacket, knowing I was going to melt in the heat outside, and said, "I'll go and see her. While I'm gone, I want you to check through the rest of the files and see if you can see anything that could link them. Maybe I missed something that you'll pick up. I'll be back as soon as I can."

27

It was obvious Adele Preston had not bought the house because of its architectural allure. It was a basic square house on a square block with no koi pond or Venus de milo statue smiling down at me coyly.

I walked along a dirt path forged through the weeds and rang the bell. Then I waited. And waited. I started to think nobody was home but I rang the bell again anyway. Still no response. I glanced towards the carport. There was no car there but that was consistent with what Queensland Transport had told me.

I stood for a few moments listening to the silence. I'd just turned, about to walk back to the car, when I heard a door bang out back. I rang the bell again thinking that Adele Preston had been out in the back garden and hadn't heard anyone at the front door. I waited again but there was still no answer.

A banging door has a sound all its own. When there is no answer at the front door and you hear that sound, it suggests all kinds of things and none of them is good.

I walked to the side of the house and saw two wheelybins sitting on a small uneven concrete path that led to the rear of the house. The house was a small three bedroom, one bathroom home so it took only seconds to walk to the kitchen door. It opened inwards and it must have had a spring that was weak because every puff of wind was blowing it open. Then the wind would die away and the door would close again with a bang. It banged three times while I stood and watched. The deadlock hadn't been engaged so it was in a permanently unlocked position as if the owner were just going out to do something in the back yard, like putting clothes on the line. Except there weren't any clothes on the line.

I pushed the door open with my elbow and stepped into the kitchen.

"Hello! Is anyone home? " I called out. "Mrs Preston?" Silence. "Are you home?"

I stood still and listened but there was no sound. No sound at all.

The kitchen smelled faintly of cooked vegetables and old coffee. Dishes lay unwashed in the kitchen sink along with the cooked vegetables draining in a colander. A dirty tea towel lay scrunched up on the kitchen bench as if it had just been used and tossed there. Except for the dirty dishes in the sink and the vegetables in the colander, the kitchen looked clean and tidy. Whatever had happened, it had been unexpected. It looked like she had been interrupted in her duties, possibly by someone she knew, because there were no signs of a disturbance.

From where I stood, I could see an archway leading from the kitchen to a hallway carpeted in a grey coloured loom, which had probably been beige at the beginning of its life. I figured it ran straight to the front door. I took a cautious step and moved slowly into the hallway as I stood my gun from my holster. Who knew if there'd been a burglary attempt and the criminal was still in side?

I crept forward, waving my gun in front of me like someone from a tacky Anne Rice novel waving a crucifix, and then stepped through the arch.

That's when I saw the dead woman lying face down on the hallway carpet, her grey hair fanning out around her head, blood pooling under her body. Her eyes were open and she had a startled, surprised look on her face as if she hadn't seen *this* coming. Her arms and legs were splayed as if she had turned to run but been stopped.

I knelt down, careful not to stand in any of the blood that looked dark and sticky, and which I guessed was about twelve hours old. I craned over to look at her face. Her eyes looked like the glass eyes of a doll and her throat had been cut, one slice that showed deep and dark. The cut was deeper on the left side, which meant that the killer had probably been left handed and had stood behind the woman as he attacked. I reached for her wrist. There would be no pulse but I checked anyway.

The murder weapon was nowhere to been seen but a dark smear of blood on the carpet suggested that the killer had wiped the blood from the knife before taking it with him. A clump of grey hair lay beside the blood and in my mind's eye, I could see it being wrenched out of her head as she tried to escape.

I stood up and backed away as I pulled out my mobile phone and called it in.

While I waited for the medical examiner and the crime team to arrive, I looked around. There were two bedrooms on the right, a lounge room and dining room combined and to the left of where the body was laying was a small impersonal room that looked like it had been used as a study because they heard that every family house should have one even if they didn't need one.

Nothing in the room had been disturbed and it didn't look like anything had been taken so it hadn't been a burglary. A small desk by one wall did not look like it had been set up for working. There were photos in wooden frames all over it. One showed a young Mr Preston and the dead woman in the hallway standing together in a marriage photo. He had been taller than her and he looked strong, handsome and vigorous. She looked petite by comparison. The photo meant that the dead woman was indeed Adele Preston.

There were several other photos showing a boy in various stages of growing and I picked up one that was of him when he was about seven years old although his eyes said he was older than that. He was standing in a backyard squinting at the camera in the sunshine with only a clothesline visible behind him. I couldn't see any toys or a bike or anything that would keep a normal 10-year-old occupied and happy.

I forced my eyes to stay looking down at the photo. This was a photo that would burn its way into my dreams and my shadows, into that part of my mind that I have no control over. Its image would reappear in all its cruelty for the rest of my life.

There was no smile on his face. His eyes were large and emotionless, as if someone had scraped off a layer of emotion the way you'd scrape the thinnest film of egg white from the shell. In those eyes were the shrivelled cast of dead hope and a closed door. They were the eyes of a brain and a soul that had collapsed under the weight of sensory overload. They were eyes of the walking dead.

I noticed his left hip was noticeably higher than his right one, suggesting he had a shorter left leg. He had a plaster cast on his right arm as the other arm hung lifelessly by his side. Just looking at his empty face made my heart lurch. What is it that psychologists say? There are none so vulnerable as those who want to be loved.

I tried to imagine him playing with action figures, gaps in his teeth and smiling, thinking life was terrific. I couldn't. That's what is so touching about children: they are usually so sure that life will be great for them. Ask any 6-year-old what they want to be when they grow up, and they will say, a doctor, a policeman, a fireman, a footballer, or maybe just rich. What had Benjamin wanted to be, I wondered? Whatever his dreams may have been, there were certainly no dreams now.

I turned the frame around so that I was looking at the back and took the photo out. On the back, it read *'Benny – aged 9'*.

I had proof of identity for the boy. I also had the dead body of the only person who could tell me what had happened ten years ago. The killer had reacted with knee jerk response.

Like people who kill every spider they see, he had killed the only person who could have identified him.

28

I walked into the squad room and Inspector Grayson was sitting at his desk on the phone saying, 'uh-huh, uh-huh, uh-huh,' and looking bored. His feet were on the desk and while he spoke, he held up a finger and crooked it to indicate he wanted me in his office.

He sat eyeing me in silence for a few moments as he tapped his pencil idly until something said on the other end of the phone caught his attention.

"Hey look, you can quote cases at me all you want but I want it clear between us," he was gesturing vigorously to make his point. "I gave your boy all the breaks I mean to give him so either he co-operates or we can put him right back where he belongs... Yeah, well, you *do* that. You talk to him. Again!"

He dropped the phone down from a height, not exactly slamming it but making his point. He dropped his feet to the floor and said, "Shut the damn door!"

I reached behind and pulled it closed, watching him all the time. He was silent for a long time. When he finally spoke, the palms of his hands were pressed firmly onto the desk enough to make his arms quiver.

"A little while ago, I had a phone call regarding a complaint against you," he said. "You want to use a life line or call a friend or can you work it out all by yourself what it was about?"

The best thing to do when the inspector is like this is to act innocent. I shrugged.

"Like you don't know, Jack," he said. He was sucking on a cigarette like it was an oxygen mask and it was his last breath. He threw his cigarette butt into a styrofoam coffee cup and lit another one. He had a voice that was perhaps weeks away from throat cancer. He made a hacking noise that sounded like Sherlock gakking up a fur ball. The cough settled to a phlegmy wheezing.

"You had a little five minute McInterview with Preston yesterday, did you not?" he continued. Lights seemed to fluoresce on his bald head while an angry expression travelled across his face. "Well, Preston called Complaints, they called the Police Chief and he called me. A daisy chain. And guess what? You're a celebrity."

Once again, veins stood out on his forehead and the thought crossed my mind that today may be the day I'd have to perform CPR on him. He took a few breaths and seemed to get himself under control.

"Do the words 'civil suit' mean anything to you, Jack? Because those words keep floating in front of my eyes. You can't go accusing someone of a crime with nothing to back up that accusation. You know that as well as I do."

"It's no coincidence that the bones show old fractures and his wife took the kid and left," I stated.

"Coincidences we leave to the astrologists. We have to deal with facts."

He took his foot off the wastebasket, and leaned forward, smoke floating in a cloud behind him as if his coat were alight. "Okay. Bring him in for questioning. We may have to charge him to keep upstairs off my back."

After my outburst yesterday at Preston's flat, I didn't relish the thought of admitting to Grayson that I'd dropped Preston from my suspect list.

I took a deep breath before saying, "I don't think he did it. He's guilty of abuse, of that I'm sure, but the murders...well...I doubt it."

"Christ Jack! Make up your mind! I'm trying to salvage a delicate situation here. Just bring him in and we'll go from there!"

"I think that's a big mistake, boss." I leant over and picked up his nameplate and turned it towards me. I then turned a picture frame with a photo of a fiftyish woman and two kids smiling away from him. "This is you at your next press release. *I'm Inspector Grayson and I've called this press conference to announce that the Surfers Paradise Police Department has been responsible and successful in the apprehension of one of the most vicious killers the Gold Coast has ever seen!*'

Grayson leant back further, his fingers tented over his round belly. "Sounds okay so far."

"Then it goes like this.... 'Ladies and Gentlemen. I'm Inspector Grayson. A few days ago, a young boy was drugged and brutally murdered. A suspect was apprehended, interviewed and charged due to political pressure, despite protests from the incredibly handsome and charming arresting officer, Sergeant Jack Curtis, previously from Hobart Police Sta.....'"

Grayson cut me off as he sat forward. "That's enough," he yelled. Veins stood out on his forehead and his face had turned a pale crimson. "Okay. Okay. Explain to me why you don't think it's him. I heard you found the body of his wife this morning. Why do you think he didn't do that? He wanted to shut her up so she wouldn't tell us about the abuse. He had motive and he certainly had opportunity."

"I just think it's too early to charge him. If we say he killed Benjamin, we have to assume that he killed the other boys as well. Am I right?"

"And what's so strange about that?" His voice sounded exasperated and I didn't blame him. I was feeling much the same myself.

"I don't think he has the brains to do this. He's a thug who beats up on a kid for a power kick but that's it. He didn't mastermind anything like murdering the other boys on the same day of every year for the past six years. That's too precise and besides, he's probably been drunk non-stop for the past ten years."

I took a deep breath. "He told me he had no idea where his wife went with the boy."

"Oh, and he's Mother Teresa who would never lie to a policeman?" He sat down heavily in his chair. "Give me a break, Jack. I've got upstairs telling me to wind this up and he practically told you he killed the boy."

"Practically being the operative word," I stressed.

"Make this work, Jack, because I've got him down for doing this. Who else is there? Tell me that. Who else?"

I had no answer for him. All I had was a gut instinct that told me he hadn't killed the other boys and since I believed all the killings were connected, it meant he didn't kill his wife either.

"Get someone to go and pick him up. We'll take it from there. As soon as he's here, I'm giving a press release that we have a suspect in custody. We have to wind this up."

"That's too soon. You'll regret this Inspector."

"That's the way it is." He leant forward and pulled the ashtray close, shaking a cigarette out of the packet at the same time in one fluid motion. He looked up at me and said, "You've got one more day to tie it all up."

I snorted. "I need more time than that."

"I don't think you've got too much time."

"What do you mean?" I frowned.

"They want you off the case."

"*They?* Who's *they*?"

"They. Everybody. The Police Chief. Complaints Departments. Shit, I don't know. Anybody else you've pissed off that I don't know about?"

I just stared at him.

"Call me this afternoon after he's in custody."

29

Tamborine Mountain was quiet, the air hot in the midday sun. I'd left Sam to organise John Preston's arrest. I had other things on my mind.

I was hoping to avoid both the morbidly curious and the media doing follow-ups on the previous day, and I had. Cars meandered their way up the mountain but none stopped and gawked or even seemed aware of the crime scene probably because the police had removed the network of tape and ramps that led to the crime scene. This was the way I wanted it. I wanted to be as close as possible to the way it was when Benjamin Preston had been dragged down the gully.

I stepped out of the car and walked to the rear, opened the lid of the boot and looked in. Lying in the trunk was a test dummy I'd borrowed from the lab that was used on occasion in the re-staging of crimes, particularly suicide jumps and hit-and-runs. They had an assortment of sizes ranging from infants to adults and adding or removing one-kilo sandbags from zippered pockets on the torso and limbs could manipulate the weight of each dummy.

The dummy in my trunk had no face and in the lab, Walt and I had removed sandbags to make it weigh 30 kilos, the estimated weight Walt had given to Benjamin. The dummy wore a backpack similar to the one recovered during the excavation.

I grabbed the dummy by its upper arms and pulled it unceremoniously out of the trunk. I tossed the dummy over my shoulder and made my way down the path through the bush to where Benjamin's body had been found. Gouges had been made in the soft dirt from where the medical examiner's people had carried him out.

I fell twice in the first five minutes and I didn't see a small leafless branch until it raked across my cheek, cutting it open. I cursed under my breath but kept going. About fifty feet from the car, I took my first break, dropping the dummy on the ground and then sitting on its chest. I pulled the front of my shirt out of my pants and used it to wipe the blood away from my cheek. The wound stung from the sweat that was dripping down my face.

"Okay, Benjamin," I said when I'd caught my breath, "let's go."

For the next twenty feet, I dragged the dummy down the slope. The progress was slower but it was easier than carrying the full weight.

After another break, I made it the last twenty feet to the spot where Benjamin had been found. I dropped to my knees and sat back on my heels.

"Bullshit," I said while gulping breath. "This is bullshit."

I couldn't see John Preston doing it. He would have been maybe fifty at the time that he was supposed to have accomplished this feat and he was not a fit man. I was also sober, something that Preston would not have been.

Even though I'd been able to get the body to the burial spot, my gut instinct told me that Preston hadn't done it. He either didn't take the body up the hill at all or he'd done it with help, which bought me back to Adele Preston. I could see the two of them carrying the body up here but not just one of them. The other boys were different. According to the coroner's report, the five other boys had been buried alive. They would have walked, or staggered most likely, only to be thrown into a prepared grave.

I stared at the spot for a few moments then looked around, not knowing exactly what I was looking for. I had precious little to work on and the criminologist had already catalogued everything the previous day. Still....

My breathing had finally returned to normal and I began backtracking my way back up the trail. Taking the dummy up the incline was harder than taking it down but that wasn't part of the test. I grabbed the arm of the dummy and dragged it up the hill to the car without falling. When I reached my car, Dr Germain was standing there with Caesar on a leash. I quickly went to the trunk, dumped the dummy in and then slammed it closed. Germain came around to the back of the car.

"Sergeant Curtis." He looked in the trunk but didn't ask what it was I was doing.

"Doctor Germain. How are you?"

"Better than you, I'm afraid. You've hurt yourself again. That looks like a nasty laceration." He grinned. "You have a dangerous job, my friend."

I touched my cheek. It still stung.

"It's fine. It's just a scratch. How's Caesar these days?"

"I don't let him off the leash around here any more. You had better come with me to the house where I can butterfly that cut. If you don't, it will scar."

I nodded and followed the doctor down to his back office and sat down while the doctor cleaned the cut and then used two butterfly bandages to close it. While he patched me up, I filled him in on the last couple of days. He listened quietly while I talked.

"I think you'll recover," he said, patting my shoulder. "I don't think your shirt will, though."

I looked down at the shirt stained with blood. I'd have to go home and change before heading back to the station.

"Thanks for fixing me up, Doc. Sorry to interrupt Caesar's walk."

The doctor shook his head in genuine distress.

"It's funny sometimes how things go," he said. "Chain reaction. First another boy dies and then the mother of the first boy dies. All because a dog fetched a bone. A most natural thing to do with the most unnatural of consequences."

All I could do was nod. Germain looked down at his dog who was lying in the spot next to the desk chair.

"I wish that I'd never taken him off his leash," he said.

"I don't know about that, sir," I said. "I think if you start thinking that way, you'll never be able to go out your door again."

We looked at each other and exchanged nods. I turned to the door but Germain stopped me.

"On television, they said the police are making an arrest in the case."

I looked at him from the doorway.

"Don't believe everything you see on TV, doctor."

30

Every trace of Adele Preston's life had been scoured from her body. Not clean like when you wash your hands. Clean like you've been scrubbing and your hands are wrinkled and raw.

During the autopsy, Walt had cut around her neck slightly above the laceration. His own incision had now been sewn back up but the knife wound remained, cleaned of blood. It had a look of plastic about it but the sharp medicinal odour that burned my nostrils told me it wasn't.

Her face was round and her lips were small and colourless. If I touched her, I knew her skin would feel chilly and hard. Her grey hair was parted in the middle and left long and shaggy which made me think she would have wound it up in a bun every day. When I leaned forward, I could see the split ends.

We cover corpses for the same reason we go behind walls to carry out our bodily functions. Some human situations cry out for privacy and being dead is one of them. Respect is called for. Not for the body, but for the person they once were.

I took a deep breath and pulled off the covering, so that only her feet were still hidden. I felt as though a bullet had punched through me again, taking with it something that no doctor could put right. It was as if the sight of her body was pouring into my skull and fixing here. Her hands were plump and somehow, it was those that moved me most. They still looked soft, as if they could curl and hold even as she lay dead on the steel table. Her legs were unshaven and her arms were downy. A scar on her left knee looked old, as if she'd fallen over when she was little and it had healed badly.

"No surprises here, Jack. She didn't die of a heart attack," Walt said.

There was a long incision down from her neck to her pubic hair that wasn't quite straight. There was a little cut around her belly button, like a road forking at an ancient monument. The wound had been neatly sewn up, like a demonstration in a home-economics lesson.

"She had liver damage and in a few years, she would have been a candidate for lung cancer but none of that is relevant to her death. She died from loss of blood due to a wound that cut her jugular vein and severed her throat."

I tried to concentrate on the relevant wound. Her throat was neatly and efficiently cut, side to side, but there were also little cuts to her hands and a couple on her arms that could have been defensive wounds. I already knew what the autopsy report would say.

Enough. I pulled up the sheet and made sure it entirely covered her body.

It was uncharacteristically quiet in the autopsy room. I don't suppose there was much to say. Perhaps I was radiating enough hostility to discourage conversation. I've always found the emotional fallout hard to take. I wanted to say something, anything to break the silence, but I couldn't think of anything so I cleared my throat loudly instead.

"Finished?" Walt asked.

"Yep," I nodded.

"Nothing you wouldn't have found in the report, Jack." Walt walked over to the stainless-steel sink and picked up a bar of soap and lathered his hands.

"I know. I just wanted to look at her body. I don't know what I expected to find."

"What'd you do to your face?" he asked, glancing at me over his shoulder as he dried his hands.

"It's just a scratch," I said. Three days back on the job and I had opened the wound on my stomach and sliced open my face. "What about the time of death?" I'd been trying to work Preston in the mix.

"She'd been dead for twelve hours before you found her. I'd put the time of death at around 9 o'clock last night." He tossed the towel into a basket that I knew would be taken out later for laundering. "I'm finished with her. You can tell her relatives the body is ready for release."

"I'm not sure there are any except for the husband who's a suspect in the murder." I smiled sadly. "Most women and men spend their lives on earth without distinction. They are born, they exist for a time with all their particular loves and dreams and pains, and then they die. And barely anyone notices. Sometimes I wonder if they may as well not have been born at all."

"The people you're talking about might disagree."

"I'm sure they would." I smiled sadly. "But who would listen."

"Worthy lives are not necessarily distinguished lives. Take a grandparent for instance. He or she may not have done anything major in their lives but they will be remembered forever by their family."

I nodded. "I can't help but wonder if I hadn't found her, how long she would have lain dead on the floor before she was found."

His eyes were dark in the wash of fluorescence from the ceiling. "We'll never know." He took the green cloth cap off his head and tossed it with the towel in the basket. "I'm off. You'll get the report by tomorrow. In the meantime, if you find a relative, let me know, otherwise the state will have to bury her."

He waved his fingers at me dismissively as I left.

31

Every cop knows that you have to get the subject to talk and give him a chance to lie on the record because most people hang themselves. There are usually three reasons why people talk.

One, they're arrogant.

John Preston wasn't arrogant.

Two, they're scared.

John Preston sat before me showing no emotion except resignation.

And three, they're not very bright.

I think we had touchdown.

I identified the occupants of the interview room as Detective Sam Neil, Detective Peter Bridgman and myself and announced the time and date into the tape recorder. So far, he hadn't asked for a lawyer so I put a waiver form in front of him on the table and reminded him of his rights once more. He glanced through it, signed it and pushed it to the side.

"Would you like a glass of water before we start, Mr Preston?"

He ignored my question. "How long is this going to take?"

"That depends on what you have to tell us."

"Water is fine," he mumbled.

I nodded to Pete and he pushed himself off the wall he was leaning against and walked out of the room. Sam sat silently beside me not saying a word but I could feel the anger radiating off her like a heater.

"Detective Bridgman is leaving the room," I said for the record.

I turned my attention back to John Preston. "Mr Preston. Yesterday afternoon you told Detective Neil and myself that you didn't expect to ever see your son again after your wife took him from your custody in 1994, is that correct?"

"Yes." He shuffled his rear end around in the chair, getting a little more comfortable.

"Okay. Let's start with the basic questions. Did you cause the death of your son, Benjamin Preston?"

Pete Bridgman walked in and placed a plastic cup in front of John Preston who took a gulp.

"Detective Bridgman has re-entered the room," I said. "Mr Preston. Would you please answer the question?"

"No, I did not." He said it without hesitation. "And this is harassment. I'm going to make another complaint."

"Be my guest." I smiled, showing him all my teeth. "Do you know who did?"

He shrugged his shoulders. "All I will say is he was alive when my wife took him."

He raised his head and looked at me, happy with his answer.

"Okay," I said slowly, like I was actually considering his answer. "When was this?"

"January 2014. I think that's about right. You people probably know more than I do."

"Please just answer the questions to the best of your ability, Mr Preston." I tried to keep my voice neutral, as if this man before me wasn't everything rancid in this world.

"I told you all this before," he said, taking another sip of water. "Do I have to keep saying it?"

I ignored the remark. "How was he when he left your house?"

I didn't expect to see his reaction to my simple question. His face seemed to collapse in on itself. I imagined sitting in the room for hours while I pressured him into admitting his crime. We'd only been in the room for ten minutes. I had to keep the pressure up.

I sat forward resting my forearms on the table. "Did you hit him?" I asked.

"Yes," he whispered. The word hung heavily in the room.

"Louder please."

"YES."

I sat back. "Where did you hit him?" I asked.

"I can't remember."

The words were spoken hesitantly so I knew he was lying. We all did. I felt something clench in the centre of my chest and then just as suddenly unclench and fill with a gust of chilled air from the air-conditioning. His answer seemed to hollow out my insides like flick of a knife.

"On the head?" I asked. I could swear the voice that came out of my mouth wasn't mine.

"Probably," he shrugged. "Like I said, I don't remember."

"What did you hit him with?"

He frowned. "What do you mean?"

Sam mumbled something under her breath.

"Did you hit him with your fists or did you hit him with an object?" I asked, giving Sam a look to quieten her.

"I can't remember," he answered, sucking in his bottom lip. "I was drinking at the time. I think it was something in his room. I remember picking up a lamp, but I'm not sure."

I blinked. "A lamp?" I waited for that one question to settle in his mind. "You hit a child with a lamp?" Again silence. "Why did you hit him?" I growled.

His hands rose to hide his face and as his shoulders rose and fell jerkily, tears dripped from beneath his palms onto the table. I waited in silence until he dropped his hands back to his lap.

"Mr Preston," I repeated. "Please answer the question. Why did you hit him?"

His hands hid his face again as the tears flowed. I waited until he dropped his hands.

"One more time, Mr Preston. Why did you hit him?"

"He...he should have been at the church. He wasn't. I got mad because I paid good money for him to go to the classes."

"You said January, Mr. Preston?"

He nodded. "Yeah. It was well after New Years Day and they were just about to go back to school from the holidays. Catholic schools go back later than public schools."

"That would have been during the school holidays. What sort of classes were they?"

"He was training to be an altar boy and he had to go there for the whole week or we'd lose the money. He should have been there and all this wouldn't have happened." He took a couple of shaky breaths. "I started to yell and I hit him and then...I was drinking hard so I don't really remember."

"Did you and your wife attend this church on a regular basis?"

He nodded.

"What was the name of the church?"

"The Sacred Heart at Clear Island Waters."

"When Benjamin didn't turn up for the classes, didn't someone contact you to find out the reason why?"

He nodded. "The priest did."

"What was the name of the priest?"

"Father Aspendale."

"And what did you tell the priest?"

He turned his head slowly to look at me and his gaze was steady. He held the look for as long as he could, long enough for the sweat to slide down his face by his ears. Eventually he looked down at the floor and took a deep breath.

"At the time, I told him Benjamin was sick."

My ears pricked up. "What do you mean... at the time?"

He took another sip of water. "The next week, I told him what had actually happened in the confessional."

The confessional. Memories of my own childhood with rigid rules and formidable priests bubbled to the top of my mind. "And what did he say?"

"He said that if Benjamin was seriously hurt that I should do the right thing by the boy and go to the authorities even if it meant they took him off us."

"And what did you do?"

"Adele didn't come back so I thought she'd just decided to leave me and take him away with her. I didn't know what had happened. She never let me know."

I stared at him silently for a few moments letting him know that I thought his excuse was pathetic. He looked up at me and must have seen the contempt in my eyes because his own eyes dropped to the table and his hands clasped each other tightly. "I told you I rang Children's Services and let them know she took him."

"But you didn't tell them about the beating, did you Mr Preston?"

His chin trembled as he shook his head.

"Where was your wife at the time you were thrashing Benjamin?"

He flinched at my choice of words but this wasn't a personality contest and I didn't care what he thought. Out of my peripheral vision, I could see Sam sitting very still and silently glaring at him. You'd have to have known Sam for a while to realise how angry she was. She's one of those people whose anger you can gauge by the reduction of movement.

"She came in from work during the fight. *She's* the reason I..."

I put my had up to stop him. "Please," I interrupted. "Just answer the question." I had a feeling he was going to start blaming his wife for his drinking and conveniently blame her for everything. I had no wish to listen.

I glanced down at my notebook where I'd written the questions I wanted to ask. "What happened after she came home?"

"She flew at me, screaming. She tried to stop me but I had this rage." He looked at me pleadingly. "I can't seem to control myself when I've had a few drinks and..."

I didn't let him finish. "What happened then?"

"She picked Benny up and ran to the door. I tried to stop her but she said she was leaving and taking Benny with her. Said she was going to take him to a hospital," he whined.

"So you knew Benjamin was seriously hurt?"

"Maybe," he whispered again.

"Did you go with your wife to the hospital?"

"No." He continued looking down at his hands.

"And why was that?'

Twin spots of defeat were imprinted in his eyes as if he'd been expecting this for ten years. As if you either have winner's luck or loser's luck and he'd always known he'd find himself in a police station with policemen waiting to put him in goal. Tears spilled from the corners of his eyes, slid down his face and were lost in his beard.

"I was scared," he said as he ran the back of his hand under his nose. "He was real still."

This was the important part. I needed a clear and simple confession of Benjamin's death. It needed to be solid and detailed enough so that it would stand up to any lawyer that Preston would later obtain. More times than not, a confession was withdrawn after a lawyer was hired. My duty was to make sure this confession stuck when it ended up in court.

"Mr Preston, are you comfortable talking to me?'

He frowned. "Yeah. I guess."

"You don't feel threatened in any way?"

"Are you going to hit me?"

I snorted in disgust. "And you are talking freely to me?"

"I said yeah, didn't I?"

"Okay. What happened when your wife came back from the hospital with Benjamin?"

"I TOLD YOU SHE DIDN'T COME BACK," he yelled. "I NEVER SAW THEM AGAIN."

I stared at him icily and he quietened down at the intensity of my stare.

"What about your son?" I asked.

"Him neither," he whispered.

"Did you make a missing person's report?"

"Why should I? Benjamin was with *her*."

I stared at him in silence for a while. Silence affects people in different ways. My silence made him feel nervous and awkward, as I knew it would.

"I want to know the truth, Mr Preston." I felt as numb as I'd ever felt, as if I'd been cored clean of emotions a swiftly as you core an apple. "Was Benjamin already dead when your wife left with him? After you'd beaten him with a lamp?"

About now, he would be wondering what I knew and how much I knew. He'd be thinking should he risk a lie or just come out with the truth and get it over with? I watched him some more as thoughts ran across his face.

He raised his eyebrows at me. As I watched, an icy realisation billowed in his eyes. "No!" he said without hesitation. "He was quiet but I could see him breathing... sort of quick little breaths. But he was alive."

"So you and your wife didn't bury Benjamin in a grave at Mount Tamborine?"

I could see the question startled him. He blinked a few times and frowned. " Wha..? No. What are you talking about? He was alive when he left. I swear. Ask her. She'll tell you."

I felt the first tremor go through me. He had no idea his wife was dead. You can't fake something like that. Something always shows in their face. They think they're being smart but something always gives them away. Sometimes it's as simple as a sideways glance before they answer. Sometimes it a subtle look that seems to say, 'I'm smarter than you'. But Preston was far from smart and I'd bet my career on the fact that he didn't know. I studied him trying to figure out which way to go from here. I had to be careful.

"You haven't seen the news today, Mr Preston?"

"I don't watch the news. It's always bad."

I waited and watched his face for a moment to see if something would show. Preston looked from me to Sam and back again, confusion on his face, but said nothing.

"I'm sorry to be the one to tell you, but your wife was found dead in her house this morning. She was murdered."

His eyes popped open and his mouth formed a perfect O just before he jumped up, knocking his chair over. Beside me, Sam gave a startled yelp and Pete stepped quickly away from the wall, ready to intervene if necessary.

"SIT DOWN, MR PRESTON," I said, standing up to face him. "Do it

RIGHT NOW!" I picked up the chair and threw it back at him. It skidded across the floor and landed upside down at his feet. Keeping his eyes on me, he bent down and picked up the chair, righting it before sitting back down again.

Most of my life, I've done a good job of staying away from macho histrionics. I could handle myself in a violent confrontation, I was sure, and that was enough for me because I was just as certain that there were always people meaner and tougher and faster than I was. And they were only too happy to prove it. So many guys I'd known from childhood had died or been jailed or, in one case, become a quadriplegic because they needed to show the world how mean they were.

So why I needed to show this scum who the boss was escapes me. I knew that Benjamin Preston's death bugged me and maybe that was a huge part of it. But more simply than that, I think, was the dawning realisation over the last year that I'd lost my taste for my profession. I was tired of people and their predictable vices, their predictable wants and dormant desires. And I was sick of the pathetic stupidness of the whole damn human species.

John Preston sat still and ran his palm over his mouth several times, blinking rapidly and breathed heavily through his nostrils. "Murdered?" he asked quietly.

"That's correct. At around 9 o'clock last night. Where were you around that time last night, Mr Preston?"

The question caught him off guard. His eyes opened wide again and he inhaled sharply when he knew where I was headed.

"Hey! I didn't do it"! Anger had returned to his eyes. His whole body was beginning to quiver with rage. The red of his eyes had darkened and his chin was pointed out straight and unyielding. "You think you're so damn smart. You're like a bloody dog running around with your nose on the ground, sniffling through bushes and piles of shit until you find what you think you're looking for. Then you step back and let the hunters shoot it dead."

It wasn't the analogy I would have chosen, but it wasn't entirely false no matter what I wanted to think.

Preston sat back unsteadily and looked at me as I held his dark eyes.

They had the odd mixture of terror and resilient bravery of a cat backed into a corner. It's the look of the crumbling soul trying to pull it all together for one last worthwhile breath.

His eyes looked from Sam to me and back a few times more, looking for something he wasn't going to find. "I don't even know where she lives anymore!"

I held his wild eyes and willed mine to be calm and flat. "I'll repeat the question. Where were you last night, Mr Preston?"

"I was at the pub with Bill. You met Bill. He was the one who told you which room I was in. I was with him. You can ask him."

"We will, Mr Preston. Don't worry about that."

Suddenly his face collapsed and he clamped his teeth down on his lower lip as tears rolled from his eyes and his shoulders shook. "I didn't mean for all this to happen," he sobbed. "I did things I'm sorry for but I was just confused."

I stood up and turned to Sam.

"Detective Neil, book Mr Preston for the wilful endangerment leading to the death of Benjamin Preston." I turned back to John Preston. "There is no confusion in a court of law when it comes to physical abuse resulting in death, Mr Preston. I would suggest you get yourself a lawyer. If you don't have one, Detective Bridgman can arrange a court appointed one for you. Interview terminated."

I pressed the stop button of the tape recorder and left the room.

32

Inspector Grayson called just as I put the final words on my report.

"I thought you were going to call me after you made the arrest and interviewed Preston."

I closed my notebook and pressed 'save' on the computer while I held the phone between my ear and my shoulder.

"Sorry. I forgot."

"What's wrong with you, Jack?" His voice was softer than I've ever heard it. "I don't think I've ever seen a detective more upset about an arrest before."

"That's because Preston didn't do it."

"Repeating something over and over does not make it true."

"That's pretty deep, sir."

Grayson was uncharacteristically quiet.

"What does Sam think?" he finally asked.

"I think she's happy to pin it on him. She's pleased to clear the case."

"We all are, Jack." There was a deep sigh over the phone. "But not if it's the wrong guy. Have you dug up anything concrete? Anything to back up these doubts?"

I touched the cut on my cheek when I remembered dragging the dummy through the scrub. The swelling was going down but the wound itself was still sore to touch. And I couldn't stop myself from touching it. It made me think of how sure I was that Preston was only guilty of causing the death of his son not the death of the other boys or his wife.

"I went up to the crime scene this morning with a dummy from the lab. I padded it to thirty kilos and I had a hell of a time getting it to the spot."

"Okay, so you proved it could be done. What's the problem?"

"*I* hauled the dummy up there. This guy Preston weighs nothing himself and you're telling me *he* carried his son up there? I was sober and it was tough! He wouldn't have been sober. I just don't think he could have done it. Not alone anyway."

"Jesus Jack! The more you talk, the more *I* sound right. So the two of them did it together. Think about it. *That's why he killed his wife.*" I heard the click of a cigarette lighter. "To stop her from telling us they were in it together."

Grayson wouldn't know that I had shrugged but he knew me well enough by now to know that I hadn't finished yet.

I heard him exhale and I imagined him sitting in his office head deep in a cloud of cigarette smoke.

"So what else, Jack?" he asked.

I took a breath before continuing. What could I say? It felt like we were burying those boys all over again. The case wasn't closed yet but it may as well be. What with the newspapers and the media release, the department had plenty of other things to worry about. I wasn't even sure is we were ever going to find this guy but I wanted to give it all I had. Those kids deserved that much.

"Preston's an asshole who enjoyed inflicting pain and severe injuries on a small boy with an impairment. But he's not our serial killer. He admitted..."

Grayson interrupted. "You can't clean toilets for a living and come home smelling like perfumed soap, Jack."

"I know what you're saying, chief, but hear me out. He admitted to hitting the boy and causing bodily damage but he insists that his wife took the boy from his custody and never returned. And I think I believe him. He just doesn't have the brains or a motive for killing the other kids.

You know the profile as well as I do. This killer is good with his hands if only because of the high degree of planning involved in these murders. This guy has a highly structured personality and he's a control freak. Not only that, but he exhibits an extraordinary level of control in the commission of his murders. That's just not Preston. I'd also expect this guy to be capable of holding down a steady job, possibly even one with some degree of responsibility and forward planning. Does *that* sound anything like John Preston to you?"

"Okay. But I also remember you saying that serial killers want to feel important and they want to feel special and they crave the sense of power and control but simply can't achieve it. Preston has a track record of child abuse which is all about power and control."

"The way this guy kills these kids and leaves them, he's very neat. Preston's a slob."

"Well, that makes me feel a whole lot better."

I ignored the sarcasm. "And this killer has to have a car."

"The killer has to have a car? That's what you're basing your investigation on? Haven't you got a better theory than that?"

"Preston doesn't have a car or a licence. And you had to see his place. It just doesn't fit any part of the profile. It's disorganised, filthy and totally wrong for a killer as precise and particular as this one is."

Grayson sighed heavily.

"I know, I know," I said before he could interrupt me. "These are just profiles and one of the dangers in profiling is closing off your mind to other options. I know all that. We could argue all day about this but I'd still come up with the same answer. He didn't kill his wife and he didn't kill those boys."

"So what do you expect me to do, Jack?" He was sounding as exasperated as I felt.

"I just need for you to give me a little more time with this. We're close. I know we are."

I heard Grayson say something under his breath and sigh deeply.

"Okay, Jack. But you've been out of the rotation now for four days and I can't afford to let you stay there. There are others who are working extra shifts to cover for you and Sam and I can't keep that happening. I know you're working the Joey Caruthers case as well as the six missing boys but the next case that comes up is yours as well. You'll be doing double the work but I can't help that. I'm sorry."

I was fine with that. "Thanks, chief. You won't regret it."

"I'd better not, Jack. I'd better not."

I hung up just as Sam walked into the room.

"He's been booked and he's in a holding cell. Pete arranged a lawyer for him and the arraignment will probably be set for tomorrow."

"Out of our hands now, Sam, but thanks." I put the report in my out tray earmarked for the inspector's desk.

"Okay, what's next?" she asked as she pulled out a chair and sat down.

I took three files and handed them to her. "We go through the files over and over and over until we find something that connects these kids."

It *felt* like there was a connection, as if somewhere there was a thread to this random violence and that if I could just figure out where that thread began, I could pull on it, unravel everything and make sense of it.

"Let's start with the most recent one." I opened Jason Bennett's file and placed his photo to one side as I began to read aloud.

"Jason Bennett, aged 10 years old, living at Mermaid Beach with his grandmother at the time of his disappearance. Went to Mermaid Beach State Primary School. Reported missing on the 2nd January, 2023 when he didn't come back from church."

I flicked through the file, shaking my head at the same time. Sam was resting her chin on her knuckles as she listened intently to me reading. "Nothing much else here," I said. "He took a backpack with him and a spare set of clothes in the morning and never returned. No one saw him after 9 am when he left his house." I shook my head. "Not much to go on."

I closed the file and put it aside. "Who's the next one?"

Sam had already opened the first file I'd given her and it was lying open on the desk. When I'd finished reading from Jason Bennett's file, she dropped her head and began to read. "Patrick McGuire, 10 years old. Lived at Broadbeach with his father who had sole custody of Patrick after the mother ran off with the husband's best friend. Went to Broadbeach

Primary School. Disappeared on 2nd January 2022 and reported missing when he..." Sam stopped suddenly.

I glanced up from my notes when she didn't finish the sentence and saw the stunned expression on her face.

"What?" I asked, leaning over to peer at the file before her.

Her eyes were wide and shocked as she looked up at me. "He was reported missing when he didn't come home from church."

I reached over and took the file out of her hands. "Let me see that."

There was a tingling running up and down my spine as I read quickly. There it was in black and white. Disappeared on his way to an altar boy class at the church but never returned.

Something started ticking loudly in the back of my mind. "What was it that John Preston just said?" I looked up and asked Sam. "Didn't he say that Benjamin played hooky from church that day? Wasn't it something about an altar boy class?"

"Oh baby, baby," Sam mumbled as she opened the next file in front of her. "Look at this!" she yelped. "Three years ago, Malcolm Archer, aged 10 years old, living at Miami. Reported missing on 2nd January 2021 when he didn't return home from the Sacred Heart Church at Clear Island Waters where he went for a religious class." She looked up at me in shock. "Sacred Heart Church, Jack. The same one that Benjamin Preston went to."

I glanced back down at Patrick McGuire's file, scarcely believing what was in front of me, and read through it again. "The same as Patrick McGuire," I said with amazement in my voice. "The only difference with his is Father Aspendale's statement." I was flicking through the file to find the statement and confirm. I stopped when I had it and said, "He states Patrick attended the class and left at 4 pm with everyone else. But he never returned home and he was never seen again after that."

I put Patrick's file aside and quickly opened the next file. I noticed my hands were shaking and I could feel sweat popping out on my forehead.

"Cameron O'Brien aged 10 years old, living at Broadbeach. Reported missing on 2nd January 2020 when he didn't come home from a meeting at his local church."

I looked up at Sam. "Why the hell wasn't this noticed by the investigating officers at the time?"

"Christ, Jack. *We've* only just noticed it. They've all been treated as runaways."

I began flicking through the last file. "For the love of God! Same thing for William James six years ago. 10 years old living at Burleigh Heads, took a backpack and said he was on his way to church that morning but never returned home. All of them 10 years old and all on their way to…" I flicked through the other files to make sure I was right, "Yep, altar boy classes at The Sacred Heart Church at Clear Island Waters, Father Aspendale residing."

Sam had a smile from ear to ear. "We've done it, Jack. Even Joey Caruthers' father said the only places they went were the shops, school and church. Even though they lived in different suburbs, they all lived in suburbs surrounding that church. Broadbeach, Miami, Mermaid Beach. The only one that lived a little further is William James who lived at Burleigh Heads. But his address was on Christine Avenue which is right on the border of Burleigh and Miami."

She jumped up and almost ran over to her desk and pulled out a street directory from her top drawer. She bought it back to the desk and kept flicking over the pages until she suddenly came to a stop.

"What are you looking for?" I asked, watching her fingers trace through the list of Catholic Churches on the Gold Coast.

"The Church of the Sacred Heart on Fairway Drive at Clear Island Waters is the closest Catholic Church to all of those boys. The next nearest one is Saint Josephs at Labrador or The Infant Saviour at Burleigh. That would have been too far for these kids to travel on their own." She flicked through to a map and traced along the grid line. "There you go. Even though William James lived at Burleigh, his home would have been closer to The Sacred Heart than The Infant Saviour."

She looked up at me again. "There's our link, Jack."

I looked at my watch. "We've got to make time to go and see this priest before heading home. You up for it?"

"You think I'd miss this?"

33

In the glow of the setting sun, the ocean had a burnished glow. The smoky dark gold of the sky contrasted with the explosion of green, reds and yellows in the canopy of trees outside the church.

The priest paced the floor in front of two rows of boys aged between eight and twelve. All twelve boys watched him in awe. He had his arms behind his back as he gazed up at the ceiling, speaking in a booming voice that bounced and echoed all around us.

The elaborate church was large, its stucco walls and Spanish tile floor magnifying every cough and shoe shuffle. The air carried a coolness that only comes from high ceilings, marble and stone. A large wooden crucifix bearing a gold figure of Christ dominated the wall behind the altar underneath an elaborate stained-glass window. Incense and candle wax hung heavily in the air as well as the sad smell of wilting flowers and long rays of tinted sun sliced through the lead light windows leaving pools of red, green and blues on every surface. Mottled dust spun in the shafts of light that slanted through the windows and disappeared into the middle rows of the pews.

"There are churches just like this one all over the world," he said as he continued to pace. "Being an altar boy is one of sacred trust. Like the disciples were to Christ so are the altar boys to the priest. In our parish, we do not allow girls to fill this position."

I believe there is a God. Maybe not the Catholic God or even the Christian one because I have a hard time believing that anything that created rain forests and oceans and an infinite universe would, in the same process, create something as unnatural as humanity that kills small boys. I stopped praying a long time ago. The demise happened slowly in my life where my impotence to bring some people to justice overtook my feeling of integrity. Afterwards, the world went on and any contact between God and myself was severed.

The priest stopped pacing and glanced up in our direction.

"Are there any questions, boys?" he asked, watching us as Sam's heels clicked loudly on the marble floor.

There was a hushed silence as the priest's eyes turned back to the boys' faces and roamed from one to the other, not missing anyone.

"No?" He looked at them in the heavy silence. "Then you are all excused. We will meet back here at 10 o'clock tomorrow morning. God be with you."

Statues of saints lined the walls and stared at us as Sam and I walked down the aisle towards the small group listening to the priest. The boys began to leave in single file in what could only be called respectful silence but I knew that once outside the church doors, all hell would break loose as these seeming angels would turn into rampaging demons once clear of the front door.

"How can I be of service?" the priest asked, walking slowly towards us.

I showed him my badge and said, "I'm Sergeant Curtis from Surfers Paradise Police Department and this is Detective Neil. We have a few questions, if we may. You're Father Aspendale, I presume?"

He smiled. "*Monsignor* Aspendale now." He tried to keep his smile meek but I knew he'd have to confess his sin of vanity next time he went to confession himself.

I smiled back and nodded. "Monsignor." I looked back over my shoulder at the boys leaving the church. "You still hold classes for altar boys, do you Monsignor?"

He nodded. "I hold one every year at this time. Unfortunately, parishioners relocate so I am forced to hold classes to replace the boys who leave."

"How many would you lose in any one year?"

He frowned. "It varies. Three or four, I would guess."

His eyes travelled from mine to Sam and back again. "Why are you interested in my altar boys? I assume they are the reason for your visit?"

"I'd like to present you with a hypothetical case." I looked down at the stone floor then back at him again. "If a person came to you to confess a crime," I shrugged like I was searching for a crime, "murder say." I let the word hang in the air for a few seconds before continuing. "What would you tell him to do?"

The monsignor looked unmoved at my question. "Well, naturally. I'd tell him to go to the authorities. But the least I would have him do was to find a way to atone for his crime."

"How would he do that?"

"That depends on the particulars of the crime, doesn't it?"

"Okay. If a boy was killed and buried without anyone's knowledge and the person responsible for the boy's death came to you. What would you tell him?"

The priest closed his eyes slowly and reopened them. "We're no longer talking of a hypothetical here, are we Sergeant?"

I stood motionless. "No, Monsignor, we aren't. We have six boys who have been murdered and stuck in the ground and all of them were training to be altar boys at your church at the time of their death."

He stared at me in silence. "What are you suggesting, Sergeant?" he asked quietly.

"The first boy, Benjamin Preston," I saw his eyes dilate before he brought himself under control, "was killed by his adoptive father, John Preston. Whoever killed the other five boys knew where Benjamin was buried. My question to you is, did John or Adele Preston come to your confession and confess their sin?"

He took a deep breath. "The confessional vow is sacred. It has never been broken in the history of the church."

"Seriously?" I asked sceptically.

"No, it hasn't," he stated adamantly. He looked up at the statues of the saints for a second before continuing. "John Preston's grasp of the true meaning of the church leaves a lot to be desired," he said quietly. "It's like a lot of mythical imagery to him. He takes what he needs and moulds it to suit his purposes and tosses away the rest. I always felt a certain...helplessness...towards Mrs Preston and the child. He was a good boy."

"I respect the seriousness of your vow but considering the situation..." I left the sentence unfinished.

"I'd like to help you, Sergeant, but my hands are tied."

"Let me put it another way. Adele Preston was murdered yesterday but John Preston is still alive and so is the one who killed the other five boys. That just leaves you." I let that statement hang in the air before continuing. "In the last five years, did you tell anyone what John or Adele Preston told you in the confessional?"

"How many times must I spell it out to you, Sergeant? I *cannot* and *would* not talk about this to you." He hesitated and looked me in the eye. "And I would not talk about this to *anyone*."

I nodded slowly. "And yet, five other boys besides Benjamin Preston, one a year that is, have been murdered during the course of your classes. Someone had to have known the circumstances of Benjamin's death. Wouldn't you agree, Monsignor?"

He hesitated, then said, "It would seem so, Sergeant."

Sam cleared her throat. "Pardon me, Monsignor, but do you have any plausible explanation for this? Because right now, you've just admitted that you are the only one, except for the Prestons, who knew about the crime committed," she said.

His blazing eyes turned slowly towards Sam. "What are you suggesting, Detective? That *I* had some hand in this terrible crime?"

She stared right back at him, not blinking and not intimidated. She shrugged and spread her hands in the universal gesture of uncertainty. "Process of elimination, father. We're just doing our jobs which I'm sure you can appreciate."

"Well, you can look somewhere else, detective. As to who knows about my altar boy classes? Every parishioner of mine is aware of them. But then, I can vouch for every one of them as being good upright Christians who would *never* stoop so low as to kill any of my boys."

"Mmmm,' she said rocking on her feet. "Just like the Prestons? They were parishioners of yours as well, weren't they?"

Sam spoke the words meekly but behind the words were barbs that both the priest and I were aware of. This was the Sam that I knew of old and I was beginning to feel a little sorry for the priest.

His chest rose and fell as he struggled to find an answer.

"Thank you, father," Sam said with a sweet smile. "You've answered my question."

The priest's face turned a shade of dry blood but before he could say anything, I said, "I'd like a list of all your parishioners, Monsignor."

"I can't give you that!" he stuttered. "That's ridiculous! What about their privacy?"

It was my turn to smile. "Are you saying that they have something to be worried about? Or ashamed about, Monsignor?"

He looked from me to Sam and back again but said nothing.

"I'll expect that list sometime tomorrow then, shall I? If not, I will be back with a warrant."

His teeth clenched tightly together and I saw the muscles tensing in his jaw line before he spun around and walked towards the door that led to the sacristy, not saying a word.

Sam dropped her head and I could hear the beginnings of a giggle working its way up her throat. "You'll go to hell for that," she chuckled.

"I'll meet you there,' I replied. "I hope there's a bar. Come on. Let's go home. It's been a long day."

34

At 9 o'clock the next morning, I waited with the small funeral group made up of Sam, Pete and Angela Ashton, plus a small gaggle of reporters. Angela had not invited her father telling him in her own way that he wasn't welcome at this gathering. I didn't agree with her, the assignment of blame is too simple for those who remain behind, but then it wasn't my call. Everybody has a cage that keeps out the sharks and those who open the door and venture out do so at their own risk.

We stood on a sloping hillside in Southport Lawn Cemetery. Angela's place was at the end of the coffin opposite Monsignor Aspendale. We acknowledged each other briefly before the ceremony, him with a scowl and me with a curious nod.

Angela had a black umbrella open against the heat of the sun. Several open graves were scattered around the cemetery, one only metres from Benjamin's grave, ready for more burials that would be happening in the next few days. The sound of the traffic from Olsen Avenue hissed nearby spilling over the sound barrier and serenading the dead as it drowned out most of what the priest had to say before it got to me.

It was a beautiful day for a funeral. Brisk overnight winds from the Pacific had temporarily cleared the smoke from the sky sending handfuls of dry leaves fluttering down onto the grass. Even the view of Tamborine

Mountain was clear this morning as the mercury hovered in the high twenties. Cirrus clouds scudded across the upper reaches of the sky along with vapour trails of high-flying jets. To our right, a stretch of silver rooves glinted under the sun, and to our left the smells of thick sauces, garlic and freshly baked bread wafted over to us in the light breeze. You couldn't hate the city on a day like this.

The air in the cemetery smelled sweet from flower arrangements scattered over nearby graves but Benjamin's coffin carried only a couple of hand-held bunches. It was a sad comparison to the others. But what could you expect. Nobody knew him and for ten years, nobody had even cared.

The priest finished reading from his bible and threw dirt on to the top of the casket. It looked like it had been made for an adult, all polished grey with chrome handles. As far as coffins went, it was as beautiful as a newly waxed car but it was too big for those tiny bones and somehow that bothered me. It was like seeing a child in ill-fitting clothes, obvious hand-me-downs or Life Line discards. It seemed to say something about the boy. That he had always been wanting in some way. Never quite good enough.

A few of the lines of the sermon managed to drift over to me and I realised the Monsignor was talking about laying Benjamin to rest in his final resting place and residing in peace and love in our hearts forever and the greater kingdom of God having welcomed Benjamin. It made me think of the Jews and their unfaltering faith in that kingdom despite the atrocities that have been documented.

Someone I once knew read a quote to me from a book that said there are no atheists in foxholes. He laughed at the time and said "It's a lie. In fact, just the opposite is true. When you're in a foxhole, when you are face-to-face with death, that's when you know for sure there's no God. It's why you fight to survive, to draw one more breath. It's why you call out to any entity because you don't want to die. Because you know in your heart of hearts that there is no hereafter. No paradise. No God. Just nothingness."

For me, the jury is still out on that one.

A series of camera flashes burst from the three reporters as the coffin was lowered and the priest made a sign of the cross. I watched Angela say a silent prayer before turning to walk past me, heading down the slope towards the parking road. I watched her for a second, trying to decide if I should follow or leave her be.

I looked back to the burial site and the priest had gone. Angela was picking up pace so I had to decide now. I removed my jacket and followed.

As I got close, she calmly turned to me.

"Sergeant Curtis, I am surprised to see you."

"Why is that?"

"Aren't detectives supposed to be aloof, and not emotionally involved? Showing up at a funeral shows emotional attachment, don't you think?"

I fell into stride beside to her.

"Why did you claim the remains?" I asked. "Why did you do that when it was up to the John Preston to bury Benjamin?"

"Because I didn't think he would do it properly. And *Peter* was more my son than he was his. I deserted him once. I wasn't about to do it again."

We got to the road and her car was the first car parked in the small row.

"Goodbye Sergeant," she said as she reached for the door handle.

I reached the handle first and opened the door for her. "Somebody once told me that life was the pursuit of one thing."

She stopped and turned around to face me.

"Redemption," I stated. "The search for redemption."

She looked at me quizzically.

"Redemption for what?"

"For everything. Anything." I held her eyes. "We all want to be forgiven."

I saw her swallow, as though she was trying to push an impossibly large lump down her throat. She forced herself to breath evenly. She nodded and looked like she was about to say something but then she stopped. She turned and got in the car then drove away without looking back.

35

Pete Bridgman walked into the squad room and paced determinately over to me.

On any normal day, Pete was every mother's dream for her little girl. He's 6-foot-tall, athletic, his eyes a topaz blue, his hair sandy blonde and his face always has a healthy flush to it. He seems to have an endless supply of pristine suits that look like they have only just come from the cleaners.

Today was not a normal day. Today, his tie was unknotted and his sleeves were rolled up to reveal tanned forearms. As he walked towards me, he wiped his fair hair back from his forehead.

"I think we have a problem, Jack."

"Well, that's an improvement. Only one?" I quipped.

The young woman stood behind Pete looking disoriented, confused, alone and terrified.

"This is Anita Erickson," he said, turning around to allow the young woman to come forward. "She and her brother, Stephen, are over from England on holiday visiting an aunt and three hours ago, her brother went missing."

Anita Erickson ran the back of her hand under her nose and sniffled.

Her hair was uncombed and dishevelled and as she bought her hand back from her face, I noticed her nails were bitten to the quick.

"Please, take a seat," I said, indicating for her to have a seat in the chair beside my desk. Pete leaned forward and pulled it out for her.

"Can I get you anything? Coffee? Water?" I asked.

She shook her head and a small tremble rippled at the base of her throat.

"Okay," I said. "Tell me exactly what happened."

Her eyes met mine and they were vibrant with confusion and a deep encompassing fear. "We've only been out here for a week," she said with a broad British accent. "We visited our aunt in Sydney last week and we're spending the last week of our holidays here in Surfers Paradise."

She swallowed and I saw a lump travel down the length of her throat. "We were walking around and he got angry with me for looking in all of the dress shops. I was terribly annoyed and said he could go off on his own for a while if he didn't like it, so he did." She put her hand to her mouth as fresh tears brimmed in her eyes. "I shouldn't have et him go off by himself."

"How long has he been missing?" I slipped open my notebook and uncapped a pen, and began to write the time and date on the top of a new sheet. 5th January, 4.25 pm.

"About six hours. Before he left, I told him to meet me back at Charlie's at 1 o'clock and we'd have lunch. When he didn't turn up at 2, I started to get annoyed with him but then, as time went on I got really worried. I looked around but couldn't see him and by three o'clock, I knew something was really wrong so I came in here."

She closed her eyes and when she opened them, all the courage she'd been sucking out of thin air for the last five minutes was gone. She looked terrified and suddenly aware of how weak the walls we erect around our lives truly are.

"He wouldn't do this to me without a reason."

I could see Pete watching me, his eyes growing darker and darker by the minute. I knew what thoughts were going threw his mind. I had the same ones.

"Is there anybody he might have gone off with?"

She spent a good minute thinking about it, and eventually shook her head. "No."

"You had to think hard about that, Ms Erickson. Are you sure there isn't someone?"

Sitting on the edge of her seat, her skin looked honeyed by her week in paradise but her eyes looked haunted. They stared at me, dark and wide, and just watching her broke my heart.

"He met some kids at the place we're staying but he just wouldn't do this to me," she said as she shook her head.

"Even if he was angry with you?"

She looked upset by my question. "He's ten and I'm twenty. Of course, we clash. He's at that horrid age. That's why I let him have a bit of time to himself. So he doesn't feel like he's stuck with me doing what I want to do all the time."

I had a bad feeling about this but panicking her wasn't going to make things any better.

"I'll need a description of Stephen, Ms Erickson."

She nodded. "He was wearing board shorts, a white t'shirt we bought yesterday in Caville Avenue and high tops. His hair is short and blondish and a bit greasy today." Her lips trembled. "And he has a British accent."

"Do you have a photo of him?"

She reached into her bag. "I've only got his passport on me. Will that do?"

I took it from her and passed it to Pete. "Get a copy made of that, will you, Pete?"

Pete nodded as he took the passport from me and walked over to the copier.

"Height?" I asked as the photocopying machine whirred in the background.

"About five feet tall."

"Weight?"

"At a guess...40 kilos."

"Eyes?"

"Blue."

Pete handed the passport back to Anita Erickson and gave the photo to me.

She looked down at the photo in my hand. "What will you do with that?"

"Have more copies made and have policemen do a shop-to-shop in Surfers to see if anyone saw him or anything unusual concerning him. We may get lucky and someone saw him."

I finished writing all the information down and looked back up at her.

"You did the right thing to come in to see us. You can never be too careful. Even if he's just sulking somewhere, we'll find him and have a talk to him about the worry he's caused. But in the meantime, I want you to go back to where you're staying and wait for us to call you. If he turns up in the meantime, please call us. Where can we contact you?"

She seemed to sag for a second as I watched tiny tremors ripple the skin of her arms when she ran a hand through her hair. As I spoke, she kept glancing at my face as if it might reveal something to her, then looked away again when it didn't, only to come back to it a second later. She reminded me of a kid with no money standing with a group of kids who had plenty beside an ice cream truck, as if she were watching cones pass over her into other hands. Half of her knew she'd never get one and the other half held out hope that the ice-cream man might hand her one out of pity. Bleeding inside with the wanting.

"Where staying at The Surfers International, Room 301," she almost whispered.

I closed my notebook. "Okay." I turned to Pete and said, "Detective Bridgman. Would you escort Miss Erickson back to her hotel, please?"

Pete nodded and touched Anita's back, indicating he was ready to leave anytime she was. She looked up at him and tried to bring up a smile but it cracked weakly and disappeared.

"It's him again, isn't it?" Sam asked as soon as Anita Erickson was out of the room.

"He's the right age but..."

A frown creased Sam's forehead. "But what?"

"Our killer is changing again. Why did he take another boy? His pattern is to take a boy once a year on the 2nd January and he's already taken a boy this year. Joey Caruthers. Why take another one?"

Sam was staring at Stephen's photo. "But something went wrong with Joey's death, Jack. It wasn't the way the killer wanted it to be."

I nodded slowly as I thought. "That's right. Joey was dumped further down the mountain but that was only because we were at the original grave site." I looked up at Sam. "Is that somehow significant? Does burying them together have some special meaning to him?" I asked. "Why was Joey different?"

Sam was shaking her head, clearly as puzzled as I was. As we talked, Pete Bridgman walked silently back into the room and stood with his frame leaning casually against the wall, his arms crossed in front of his body, listening.

"Let's go at it again," I said, acknowledging him with a nod. "The first boy murdered was Benjamin Preston ten years ago. I think we all agree that his death started the next series of killings even though it was five years later. Something happened to the killer to make him start to kill other boys. He buried the others in a circle around Benjamin which could mean Benjamin's death had special meaning to the killer."

I felt a warm prickle begin to knot under the skin of my brain.

"They were buried in a circle around Benjamin," I repeated, realisation beginning to dawn. "They were brought *to* Benjamin."

Pete pushed himself off the wall. "Joey wasn't, though," he said. "Joey was dumped somewhere else. I read Mary's report again this morning. She says that there was a gap left in the circle around Benjamin Preston." His face paled a little as his eyes found mine. "There's still a gap there right now."

"The excavation site!" I yelled. "That's where he's headed!" Thoughts were flowing on top of one another. "He's going there to bury Stephen and he's probably burying him right now."

I stood up abruptly, almost knocking my chair over, and grabbed my coat where my car keys lay in a pocket. As I pulled them out, I said to Sam, "We've got to get there now." As I ran to the door, I called out to Pete.

"I want backup, Pete. NOW. The excavation site on Tamborine Mountain. Sam and I are on our way there now. Tell them we'll meet them there."

As we ran, a taxi cut us off, nearly clipping another group of people stepping off the curb into the abyss. I muttered a curse but kept running, glad that I'd parked the car close by.

The light on the horizon had gradually faded under a band of storm clouds and the ocean water was growing dark, turning yellow with the reflection from the streetlights that had just come on. On the esplanade itself, the lights were bright and cold against the deep shadows of the ocean. The breakers pounded on the beach and the force of the waves created a plume of spray that marched from right to left and there was a damp smell of seaweed. The salt water would have been eye stinging further out in the ocean.

Sam and I reached the car at the same time and as I was putting the keys into the ignition, Sam yanked her door closed.

My foot automatically pressed the accelerator to the floor and the car responded and sprang forward nearly clipping a suicidal cyclist riding too close to the side of my car. I cursed aloud and manoeuvred around him, glaring at him as we passed. He gave me a one-finger salute for my trouble.

"You know, we still don't know why he's killing these boys," Sam said, puffing heavily.

"I know, I know. We're missing something. Something very important. But right now, that boy is my first priority. Working out the *whys* will come later."

Time seemed suspended and in the silence I kept hearing this voice in the back of my mind saying *You're too late. You're too late. You're too late.*

For the next few minutes, I drove frantically, first travelling along Smith Street and then connecting with the highway heading towards Exit 57. They were the longest of my life. I kept driving and eventually, the exit for Oxenford / Mount Tamborine came into sight and I turned off, tyres screaming. Sam lurched with the car but said nothing as she hung onto her armrest.

As we drove, the sky had been darkening and streetlights had begun to switch on and I knew that the excavation site would be dark already with the thick cover of trees.

"Have the torches ready, Sam." I was concentrating so hard on the winding road that I didn't want to take my eyes of it for a second. Ahead in the beam from the headlights, a darkness loomed on Sam's side of the car as the road gave way to the vast valley below. Almost of its own volition, my foot came off the accelerator as a vision of us lying at the bottom crossed my mind.

Finally, the site came into view and I screeched to a halt on the side of the road, stones and dirt rising like a cloud around my car.

I grabbed a torch from Sam and ran, slipping uncertainly on the loose, uneven ground, leaving Sam behind me. As I ran, I had my gun out, pushing through a turnstile of branches that threatened to tear my shirt as my torch wavered uncertainly before me.

The site came into view and I dropped to a crouch, my gun in one hand and the torch in the other, while I leant against a tree for support.

There was nothing but silence in the canopy of trees. Absolutely nothing. And nobody.

I've heard people say that silence can be deafening and it's true. I spun around expecting to see……*someone*.

"This site hasn't been touched."

Why I whispered the words, I don't know. But they sounded reverent in the stillness. As though I was sitting in the front row of a church waiting for the service to begin. "How can that be?" I said in amazement.

Sam had stopped and was looking down at me, a strange look in her eyes. Something akin to doubt and uncertainty. "He's not here, Jack," she said.

I was shaking my head. "He has to be, Sam." My head kept turning from side to side, searching the scrub. "He has to be."

As we stood looking around, we could hear the sound of thrashing coming from the direction of our car. *Backup* I thought.

They stopped a few feet from us and I heard someone say, "What are we here for? A séance?"

Sam held up her hands to them. "False alarm. Sorry guys. Sorry."

I heard a mumbled "What?" from someone behind me before Sam

said, "Head on back to the station. We'll call it in and explain what happened before you get there."

I was aware that everyone was looking at me and that I didn't feel like myself. I felt crazed and unhinged.

The four policemen stood uncertainly looking at each other until Sam said in a stronger voice, "I said THAT'S IT! Get going."

They all turned to walk back to their cars as they talked quietly to each other. I think someone even snickered. I listened to the leaves crunching under their feet. Gradually the sounds became less and less and I was left standing in the darkness listening to the cicadas humming in the background.

"Let's go, Jack," Sam said softly as she turned and began to follow the other policemen back to the car. I tracked behind her with a thousand thoughts running through my mind.

When we reached the car, I tossed the keys to Sam. "You drive. I don't think I'm up to it."

I sat heavily in the passenger side of the car and threw the torch back into the glove box as I loosened my tie until it hung at my sternum. Sweat was running down the side of my face and I wiped it away with my sleeve.

As Sam turned the car around and headed back down Tamborine-Oxenford Road, I said, "I'm sorry, Sam. I was so sure I was right."

My eyes searched the darkness outside for an answer. I couldn't believe it. What other explanation could there be? Everything fit. There wasn't any other answer.

Beside me, Sam said nothing as she kept her eyes on the road.

A surge of anger flowed through me, forcing me to be aware of what my mind was refusing to believe. I'd let another kid down.

As we drove in silence, I couldn't shake the feeling that I was right and there was just something subtle that I was missing.

"I AM right!" I yelled.

Sam jumped in her seat and her eyes glanced across at me before turning them back to the road again. She muttered, "Jesus Jack. You want me to drive over the edge?"

"That kid is out there with the killer right *now*," I yelled again. As sudden as my anger had arrived, it went and I was left with this feeling of utter desolation.

My voice softened. "And I don't know what to do."

I sat staring out the window certainty and then it suddenly hit me like a cricket bat. I felt a bead of sweat on my top lip, tingling hot then cold. I felt so sick, my stomach felt like there were a hundred snakes in there and all of them were fighting each other.

I felt my stomach contract. "Oh my God." I sat up straight. Time seemed suspended as I stared out of the windscreen. "Wait a minute. Wait a minute," I mumbled in confusion. Bells were ringing like crazy inside my head and dozens of pieces of ignored information were clambering to the front of my brain.

"Whoever is doing this is bringing the boys to the original gravesite. Right?"

Sam nodded, not sure where I was going with this.

"To Benjamin, Sam. That's the key to this. They're bringing the boys *to Benjamin*."

Feelings aren't normally reliable and they're certainly not perfect. Cops don't catch a killer by sitting around *feeling* stuff. They collect facts not feelings. That's how you investigate. Feelings can become distorted. They're just interpretations, not a record and they're irrelevant if you have the facts. But at this moment, I knew my feelings were right.

"Of *course* he didn't take Stephen to the mountain." I turned to face Sam. "Benjamin's not on the mountain anymore. He's at the cemetery."

Sam kept driving and I could sense that she was thinking, but still doubting my reasoning.

"And the killer knew that."

Sam's sharp intake of breath meant she knew what I meant. Her breath came faster and she blinked a few times but she kept driving.

I slammed my hand on the glove box. "Come on, Sam. What are you waiting for? Turn the car around! What's the matter with you?"

"Jack," she said uncertainly. "We've just come from…" Her voice was full of doubt and confusion and she was shaking her head. I couldn't blame her. It sounded wild even to me. But I knew I was right.

"TAKE THE NEXT TURNOFF, SAM," I yelled as the Smith Road exit loomed ahead.

She hesitated briefly then indicated and veered sharply across the left lane to make the exit. Behind us, a horn blared but she ignored it.

During the next ten minutes, we switched lanes continuously and I was reminded of the dodgems at the few carnivals I'd been to in my youth. The Camry was moving fast on the road but inside it felt like time had stopped.

The exit for Olsen Avenue came into view and the car tipped a little as Sam swerved on to it without breaking. I had to push against the roof to maintain my balance. Five minutes later, Southport Lawn Cemetery came into view and as we turned, lights sprang at us from a car turning out of the entrance.

Sam yanked the wheel to the left barely missing a stonewall and we lurched to a halt, inches from the oncoming car.

"What the....." she mumbled. "Is that him, Jack?"

The driver was just a dark shadow behind the wheel.

"I can't see anything," I said as I leant forward and squinted through the windscreen. "It's too dark inside the car, but it *has* to be him."

In the movies, the hero (and that would be me) is fast, wily and strong. In a flash, he disarms the villain with a minimum of effort and pain to himself, while the bad guy is left floundering. Unfortunately, this wasn't the movies and as much as I'd like to be, I wasn't the 'Van Damme' type.

"We have to get that kid," I said as the car spun around us.

Sam had already begun to turn the wheel so that we could follow the fast disappearing car. The taillights glowed red as it sped away along Olsen Avenue towards the exit leading towards Southport.

"No, no," I yelled as I grabbed hold of the steering wheel.

Don't try this at home, kids. The driver loses all control of the steering mechanism and the car swerves erratically on any loose gravel that is covering the surface of the road.

"SHIT JACK!" Sam's eyes widened as she stopped centimetres from the looming stonewall of the cemetery. "What the hell are you doing!?"

"Stephen's not in the car, Sam," I said as my heart thumped in my chest. "He's already in the ground. That's why the killer's leaving. He's buried him beside Benjamin."

I opened the glove box again and grabbed the torch. As I jumped out of the car I yelled, "Get the station on the radio and tell them where the car was headed." I felt a drop of rain on my face. "It was a dark coloured Ford, recent make headed towards the Gold Coast Highway. Tell them to follow but don't apprehend. I want to do that myself."

I looked in all directions trying to decide which way to go. The last time I was here, the sun had been shining and landmarks had been visible. Now it was dark and I could barely see five feet in front of me. I turned my head one way and then the other, trying to pick up anything that looked familiar. Then I ran, breathing heavily, instinct telling me where Benjamin's grave was. My shadow, thrown by the streetlights, preceded me and spread raggedly across the head stones and mounds of dirt.

Time seemed disjointed and slow. One moment I was running, the next I was on my hands and knees where I'd fallen on overturned dirt. Something momentarily covered the moon and I looked up to see a cloud that would very soon open up and release the rain that had been threatening for weeks. There was a sudden zigzagging through the sky and just as suddenly, the rain began beating against my face so hard that there was nothing to see except a dense liquid fog while raindrops exploded on the ground.

I stumbled onwards, drawing on every ounce of energy. The temperature seemed to have dropped by 10 degrees in the last ten minutes. I looked up into the sky and there was just a void of emptiness as the rain came down. Every now and then, I stopped to get my bearings before running on. My chest hurt and I knew that I had taken the scab off the healing wound on my stomach again. But I held on. I held on with everything I had.

Up ahead, I could see the area where Benjamin had been buried. I felt exhausted but I thought about the boy, about how scared Stephen must be, all alone with the weight of soil pressing down on his body and his face, unable to breath or move.

Suddenly, I was there. Two graves sat side by side. One had flowers sitting on the mound of dirt and I saw my own bunch withering amongst the other two.

I turned the torch around in my hand and, using the end of it, began to scrape away the dirt from the recently filled grave beside Benjamin's.

Time seemed suspended and endless. Suddenly, toes appeared and I felt my heart lurch.

"Oh God," I said as I spun my body around and began the same process of digging at the end where Stephen's head would be. My lungs were burning and I had to keep wiping the rain away from my face to see. But I kept digging.

Within seconds, a head appeared. Dirt covered the face and filled the eyes I had no idea if the boy was alive or dead. All I could think of was to get him out as soon as I could. I burrowed my hands into the soft soil on either side of his head and felt his shoulders. Then I heaved. Inch by inch, the body came out of the loose soil and a minute later, I had him lying by the side of the grave.

He wasn't breathing. I lay my head on his chest but I couldn't feel the rise and fall of his chest. I stuck my fingers in his mouth and started pulling out dirt.

In the distance, I could hear a siren and I could see the blue lights of an ambulance coming into view. But I couldn't wait. If I didn't do something now, it could mean the difference between this boy's life or his death.

I could hear footprints pounding towards me as I breathed into the boy's mouth, trying to push air into his lungs. One of the paramedics shoved me out of the way and continued while I pulled myself off the ground and stood out of the way, puffing and wheezing.

Sam ran up and stood beside me, her high heels in her hand. "A patrol car saw the car speeding on the freeway and followed it," she said. "I have the address and the patrol car is on alert but not entering the premises as you requested."

Rain was falling steadily on her face and she blinked continuously to clear her eyes. She watched the paramedics working for several seconds before her eyes made a small darting look at me then blinked twice before returning to the small body on the ground. All of this was in my peripheral vision as I stood transfixed, watching the paramedics sit back on their haunches and turn towards us.

"I'm sorry, Sergeant," one of them said. "He's gone."

A surge of anger flowed through me, forcing me to be aware of what my mind was refusing to believe. I should have known this was where the killer was headed. Instead, I'd told Sam to drive to the excavation site on a wild goose chase and because of that hesitation, this young boy with his whole life ahead of him was lying in the rain, dead.

All of these years, I'd prided myself on instinct and when I needed it most, it was gone. Or had never been there in the first place. Sometimes it felt like I was in a bad dream that I didn't know how to wake up from.

The shadows looked a deep black and the rain shimmered bright silver and pearl. The soft patter on the ambulance was one of the loneliest sounds I've ever heard.

"Let's get going to that house," I said to Sam as I spun around and headed towards the car.

Behind me, I heard the paramedics talking softly as they walked to the back of the ambulance for a stretcher.

36

Rap played on someone's stereo and the smell of barbecued meat was fresh and strong. A couple of hours ago, children had been playing on these lawns and riding their bikes. No one had any idea that a murderer was living in their midst and had been killing small children like the ones happily playing in the misting rain.

Around us, palm trees swayed gently and lawn sprinklers spun. Laughter came from a nearby house as a dog barked forlornly in the distance. The house was a low set brick house set back from the street, rendered and painted in a colour that was fashionable ten years ago. The lawn was neat and tidy and lushly planted with trees and shrubs. A man in a striped shirt walked past us leading a small fluffy dog on a leash. He looked at me and must have seen something that I normally keep hidden because he picked up his pace with a quick sideways glance. A kid was screaming in the neighbour's yard and as I watched, I saw a young boy chasing a younger girl with a water pistol.

I waved to the two policemen in their patrol car to wait outside while Sam and I went inside alone. Both of them had their guns ready as they crouched behind the open doors of their car. Sam and I crept up to a portico overflowing with gardenias and ferns. As we approached the front door, we pulled out our own guns.

The door was ajar and everything was dark inside except for a light that shone dimly from the back of the house.

We gently pushed the door open.

Silence.

Streets lights gave the lounge room an eerie glow and even though my heart pounded in my chest and my nerves tensed; I subconsciously noted that the house was sparsely furnished. The carpet looked beige coloured and there was lots of clean wall space with no photos on the walls. It almost had an unlived-in feel to it.

Sam tensed as we both heard of shuffling noise at the back of the house and then a scraping. We both stopped, guns ready, and listened. The sound continued but it wasn't moving towards us. It just continued dull and monotonous in the background.

We moved stealthily towards the noise and the light.

I led the way past a bathroom and then a bedroom on either side of a narrow hallway before stopping a metre away from a door where a light was shining. I held my hand up for Sam to stop as well. Slowly, I moved my head so that I could see around the corner, my gun still held out in front of me, poised and ready to shoot.

I could see the back of a woman bent over scrubbing the floor. Her brown hair with streaks of grey swayed from side to side. Now and then, she moved her hand up to push it away from her forehead. I moved around the corner until my body filled the doorframe, my gun held out in front of me, pointing straight ahead. The strange hunched figure on the ground was totally absorbed in her task.

Then Angela Ashton looked over her shoulder at me and smiled.

"These boys!" she said as she shook her head from side to side. "They're so messy. They come over to play with Peter and they always leave such a mess." She bent over again and started to scrub again. "They never clean up after themselves."

While I watched, she dipped the scrubbing brush in the bucket full of sudsy water. "Just look at this," she said as she continued to scrub.

In Hollywood, there's a moment in film and television shows when a particular shot or word signifies that moment when the penny drops. Sometimes, it's something little that goes 'click' and everything seems to fall into place. For real people, it triggers something in the memory and we remember where we left our car keys or the name of that someone or that song we've been wracking our brains to think of. For Harry Callahan, it's usually a darker revelation. It's the instant that signifies the break in a case. Then when comprehension dawns, the camera zooms towards the face of the hero and the music reaches a crescendo as the light of realisation grows in their eyes.

This does not happen in real life. Even as I felt my stomach contract, even as I felt my heart turn to ice, I somehow managed to detach. I felt something in me harden. I often saw this as my strength. Ask Sally and she'll say it is my weakness.

My heart raced and my skin crawled with apprehension. Bells were ringing like crazy inside my head and dozens of pieces of ignored information were clambering to the front of my brain.

Memory is an amazing thing. Sometimes it's something as obvious as a photo that triggers the memory. Other times it's merely a scent or gesture that sends your mind in action. I should have read the signs. I should have seen this. If I had, Stephen would still be alive.

But memory is unreliable. It's not perfect. It's not even good. Cops don't catch a killer by sitting around remembering stuff. They collect facts not recollections. Facts, not memories. That's how you investigate. Memory can change the shape of a room. Change the colour of a car. Memories can be distorted. They're just interpretations, not a record and they're irrelevant if you have the facts. I'd had the facts, but didn't put them all together.

Time seemed suspended as I stared.

I felt my world flip completely off its usual course. Everything became upside down as if I was looking at a hole in the ground and I was seeing stars floating at the bottom and in the sky, trees were hanging suspended.

I dropped my gun to my side and watched Angela scrub in silence.

37

Shock can be a sudden or violent blow or it can be the result of a physical collapse or depression. It can set in after a severe injury, a great loss of blood or it can happen after a sudden emotional disturbance. As with a physical blow that weakens a person, an emotional blow will weaken a person's mind.

I sat opposite Angela Ashton, her face devoid of emotion as she looked back at me and I knew her mind was as fragile as any I'd ever seen.

"Angela. How did you know where Benjamin was buried?"

Her eyes glowered as she said, "Peter. His name is Peter."

I nodded. "Okay. Peter. How did you know where to go?"

She shrugged. "I buried him there."

Amazement must have registered on my face because a small frown appeared between her eyes.

"What?" I croaked. "*You* buried him?"

She nodded. "Adele and I buried Peter. She rang me and..." she swallowed and took a deep breath, then frowned, confused as she looked down at the table.

"Go on, Angela," I said softly. "Adele rang you..."

"Yes," she said as she looked back up at me. "She was upset and crying. She said Benjamin was hurt but I knew who she meant. She meant Peter."

Her face twisted in hate. "That *monster* hit Peter and Adele said she couldn't wake him up." She was shaking her head. "I rang so many times." Her look was intense as her eyes pleaded with mine. "So many times. But they wouldn't let me see him. And then it was too late."

She sneered. "I gave her my address. When she turned up, Peter was just lying there on the back seat of the car. *She* was crying and my baby was dead."

She looked down at her hands lying in her lap. "I didn't know what to do. I couldn't scream or cry." Her eyes grew wide as they looked back up at me again. "He was dead." She took a deep breath. "And it was all my fault."

"How could it be your fault, Angela?" I asked softly.

Her head was nodding. "It *was* my fault. My fault for letting my father give my baby away to them. It was my fault he died." She was patting her chest with her hand, stressing the point to me.

"He had no friends, you know. That's what Adele told me. He never had any friends because his leg stopped him from playing normal games with them." Her eyes widened more. "And that was my fault, too."

"Angela," I said as a mild reprove. My voice sounded tinny and faraway. "How can *that* be your fault?"

"I drank alcohol when he was inside me. And I smoked. I shouldn't have. The doctor told me not to but I knew better, you see. And look what I did. I hurt my baby." She was rocking backwards and forwards as she spoke. "Those other boys, they didn't have any friends either."

This woman kills, a voice whispered. *She killed six kids.*

"How did you meet those other boys, Angela?"

Kills, the voice whispered.

"They went to the same church I went to. I used to talk to them after the service sometimes."

"But not all of them were runaways, were they? What about Joey?"

She drugs them and ties them up, the voice hissed, *while they're still alive.*

Her eyes darted around the room. "His father brought Joey into my shop one day and I remembered him from the church as well. I got to talking to them. Joey wasn't quite right but he was so friendly." She smiled sadly, seeing something in her mind that no one else could. "He told me that he didn't have a mother and it was then that I decided to help him. None of the boys had a mother, you see."

I stood in silence as I remembered talking to Sonya Bennett talking about her daughter leaving Jason in her care years ago. I saw William James' father telling how his wife had died and William was all he had now.

Certain types of people become targets for predators. The same way that injured or weak animals are chosen as prey. Certain types of children are molested, for example. Shy ones, those who don't fit in and play away from the group. Ones who separate themselves from others because of pain.

Homo Sapiens survived by adapting to their environment. Being forced to adapt to terrible situations you've been made to survive can cause a lot of strange feelings as well as a lot of resentment and pain. These kids must have felt just that pain. My gut told me that. All of those boys separated themselves from their peers because of one fact: the pain of losing a mother.

"They all went missing on 2nd January, Angela. Why that day?"

"That was the day Peter died," she said simply.

My ears were ringing and my throat had constricted as though someone had their hands clenched around it. I just wanted to get the hell out of there but I wasn't sure where to go next. She looked human, made all the right sounds, but I knew she wasn't.

"Why did you kill them, Angela?" I asked softly.

They cry and she kills them. Then she buries them. This woman with the open face and the kind eyes murders little children.

She looked at me, surprised at my question. "I wanted to give the boys back to their mothers and I wanted to give Peter someone to play with. I wanted to surround him with friends that he didn't have when he was alive. That's the least I could do, wasn't it? It was all for him."

A sudden chill blew across my heart and a pit opened and yawned then extended from my throat to my stomach. Her words penetrated me and blossomed in my chest.

"Someone had to take care of him," she said.

I knew those simple words would haunt me forever, as if they were written in stone.

38

"It's over." I could hear the tiredness in my voice.

Sam nodded and whispered, "Thank God."

She was standing at the window watching the rain sweep across the water towards our building, the darkness almost complete except for the soft glow of the streetlights along the esplanade that made her look like a silhouette. Right now, the palm trees were so highly illuminated by the lights, they actually cast shadows on the wet surfaces. There was just enough wind to set them in motion, shaggy heads nodding together.

When the moon is full, the darkness of Surfers has the quality of a film scene shot day for night and the effect is dramatic. The sky at night isn't really black at all. It's a soft charcoal grey, nearly chalky with the light pollution. Right now, I couldn't see the ocean but I could faintly hear the reverberating rumble of the tide rolling in.

Sam always seems posed when her mind is somewhere else, although she is unaware of it. Her limbs simply fall into arrangements as her head cocks to one side. As she watched the darkness, I turned around and made my way back into the empty squad room. The room, always warm and muggy, felt cold to me.

I stood looking down at my desk littered with files, Styrofoam coffee cups, phone messages and someone's empty Chicken McNugget box. I remembered standing at the white board and telling the squad my theories. *I* was the profiler. The one who had all the theories on who the killer was. *I* told them all who to look for and I was so wrong. About everything. I should have known.

I gathered up the scattered files that had kept me awake for the past four nights and put them into my 'out' tray to be returned to archives in the morning. Old phone messages came next. After checking through them to see if any were important, I dropped them in the rubbish bin along with the coffee cups and empty food box. A folded piece of paper with Grayson's writing was sitting in my 'in' tray and it read *'Where the hell are you?'*

I studied it for a long time. It made me think about all that had happened since I started work on New Year's Day. I remember thinking at the time that most people viewed New Year's Day with a sense of hope and a new beginning, others saw it differently. I'd had no idea at the time how that day was going to affect my life and my future. It made me think about what I was doing and where I was going and it made me know the answer to the question.

"Nowhere," I said aloud as I screwed up Grayson's note. A gargoyle called guilt was riding my shoulders, head back, laughing and showing sharp teeth. A small taunting demon of guilt, whispering things that could have been done and weren't. I knew the gargoyle. We weren't friends, but I knew him well.

I cleared a space in my top drawer and folded the piece of paper in half. As I placed it in the drawer, I noticed the scratches and scars on the back of my hands and the dirt buried deep under the nails. I thought about the interior scars that no one would ever see.

The weight of the last twelve years hung behind my eyes like a pendulum. I had always known that I would be lost without my job and my badge and my mission. In that moment, I knew that I was just as lost with it as well. In fact, I was lost *because* of it. The very thing I thought I needed most was the thing that drew the shroud around me.

I felt something cleave inside and tear away, leaving a clarity: a horrible inescapable clarity. The blinkers were being lifted, and for once I could see the truth. Something can sit in front of you waiting to be noticed for what it is, and often you're sitting too close to really see it.

I think sometimes when we're old, we'll finally be settled about the things we've done, all the choices we've made, but then I wonder if we'll look back and think about all the things we could've done.

I remember when I'd first joined the force. I'd had hopes of becoming someone who could make a difference. Now I looked at my life and I felt an exhaustion that had become all too common lately; a bitterness with what I did that had taken place in my bone marrow.

I began to take stock of my life. I was 40 years old. I had a gun and a badge and I go out most days and pretend I'm actually doing something, and my concern was the fact that I'm not. I bust down doors that hide the smell of things you couldn't even begin to identify. I go through days when people shoot at me and people get killed. And then, I go home to my shitty home and eat microwave food and sleep until I have to get up and do it again. That was my life.

When I was a child, one of the nursery rhymes I hated the most was Humpty Dumpty. It's a very scary poem. Humpty falls over the edge and breaks into a lot of pieces and no one knows how to put him back together again. Not all the king's horses or all the king's men. No one. Nobody wants to think there's anything in the world that could fall apart as badly as that. Right now, I was Humpty Dumpty. I felt broken beyond repair. And when you begin to feel yourself going over the edge, all you can do is hang on to your mind tightly, like it's a rope that will swing you away, hoping only to land well away from where you are.

When you begin to feel yourself going over the edge, sanity receding from you as a boat recedes inevitably from the shore, you hang on to your mind tightly: like a rope that will transport you and swing you away hoping only to land well away from where you are.

It was at that moment I made my decision. It was time to start a new chapter in my life and it was the getting away from the present one that I was concentrating on now.

I reached into my coat pocket and took out my wallet as I blew air out through my mouth in a loud push. I slid my ID card from behind the plastic window and unclipped my badge. I ran my thumbs along the indentations and smiled when my thumbs felt the word *detective*. Next I put the badge and the ID card in the desk drawer beside my gun and looked at them for a moment before closing the drawer and locking it with a key.

I knew that Grayson would suggest counselling and that works for some people. I know society tells us it's good to talk about tragedy, to discuss it with friends or qualified strangers, and maybe so. But I often think we talk way too much in this society, that we consider verbalisation a cure that it very often is not. I'm prone to brooding as it is, and I spend a lot of time by myself which makes it worse, and maybe some good would have come if I'd discussed the last few days with someone. But I knew I wouldn't. I put things out of my mind every day in this job and *that* was how I kept my mind intact.

I stood and walked through the squad room to Grayson's office. The door was unlocked and I put the key to my desk drawer on his desk blotter. When I didn't show up in the morning, I was sure he would take the key and he would check out my drawer. It would be then that he knew I wasn't coming back. I was done.

Tomorrow, I would sleep in until midday and have a late three-hour lunch at the Grande Hotel at Southport overlooking the park, the ocean and the pelicans before heading back home with a full stomach and another early night in mind.

From my veranda, I would spend most of my time sitting and watching people until I knew what to do with my life. In the mornings, I will carry my coffee and sit in the cooling air and look across my yard at the back of the local school. I'll watch the small boys in their blue ties and matching pants and the small girls in their blue pinnies and berets shrieking during endless supplies of frenetic energy and I hope the memory of what it is like to feel whole will return.

As I walked back through the squad room, I felt an air of finality move through me. But I didn't hesitate. I passed the front desk and opened the heavy front door of the station. It was a warm, wet night and there was no sign of a moon in the cloud cover. The rain had varnished the streets perfuming the air with a smell of wet palms and bark.

Unless Sherlock had decided to drink them, I knew there were two beers waiting in the fridge for me at home.

I walked in silence through the heavy fog to a cab rank as misty rain fell steadily.

www.ingramcontent.com/pod-product-compliance
Lightning Source LLC
Chambersburg PA
CBHW072153070526
44585CB00015B/1127